Research & Professional Resources in *Children's* Literature: Piecing A Patchwork Quilt

Kathy G. Short, Editor
University of Arizona, Tucson

INTERNATIONAL READING ASSOCIATION
Newark, Delaware 19714, USA

The International Reading Association attempts, through its publications, to provide a forum for a wide spectrum of opinions on reading. This policy permits divergent viewpoints without assuming the endorsement of the Association.

Director of Publications Joan M. Irwin
Managing Editor Anne Fullerton
Associate Editor Christian A. Kempers
Assistant Editor Amy L. Trefsger Miles
Editorial Assistant Janet Parrack
Production Department Manager Iona Sauscermen
Graphic Design Coordinator Boni Nash
Design Consultant Larry Husfelt
Desktop Publishing Supervisor Wendy Mazur
Desktop Publishing Anette Schütz-Ruff
Cheryl Strum
Proofing David Roberts

Library of Congress Cataloging in Publication Data

Research and professional resources in children's literature: piecing a patchwork quilt/Kathy G. Short, editor.
    p.   cm.
    "Aimed at elementary and middle school contexts, specifically preschool through grade 8 (age 14)"—Introd.
    Includes bibliographical references (p.   ) and index.
    1. Children's literature—Research—Bibliography.   I. Short, Kathy Gnagey.
Z1037.A1R46
[PN1009.A1]   1995   94-43802
011.62—dc20   CIP
ISBN 0-87207-126-X

Coauthors

Betsy Brown
Margaret Jane Ferguson
Lauren Freedman
Cyndi Giorgis
Sandy Kaser
Julie Laird
Rena Leith
Prisca Martens
Janelle B. Mathis
T. Gail Pritchard
Jean S. Schroeder
Elaine G. Schwartz
Kathy G. Short
Terri L. Tarkoff

All of the coauthors are associated with the
Department of Language, Reading & Culture in the College
of Education at the University of Arizona in Tucson.

About the Authors

Betsy Brown teaches fourth grade in Sierra Vista, Arizona. She is completing her Ph.D. with a major in reading and a minor in children's literature. She also teaches children's literature to preservice teachers.

Margaret Jane Ferguson taught first grade and is now teaching a multi-age first and second grade class at Corbett Elementary School in the Tucson Unified School District. She has completed her master's and is working on a book about her social studies curriculum based on her own teacher research.

Lauren Freedman teaches 7th and 8th grade Language Arts at Townsend Middle School in Tucson Unified School District. She is also working on her Ph.D. with a focus in children's and adolescent literature.

Cyndi Giorgis is a recent Ph.D. graduate in children's literature and library science. She is currently co-director of the Tucson Library Power program and is an Adjunct Professor at the University of Arizona in children's and adolescent literature. She is on the Editorial Board for the Children's Book Column of *The Reading Teacher*, on the Advisory Board of *Book Links,* and is Associate Editor of *The New Advocate.*

Sandy Kaser recently completed an Educational Specialist degree with a focus in children's literature. She teaches a multi-age fourth and fifth grade at Robins Elementary School in the Tucson Unified School District where she conducts classroom research and supports teacher study groups to foster professional growth.

Julie Laird teaches kindergarten and Reading Recovery at Cragin Elementary School in the Tucson Unified School District. She is a doctoral student with a focus on emergent literacy.

Rena Leith has a master's in English Literature from Purdue University and a Ph.D. from the University of Arizona with a focus in English Education. Her interests include literary theory, educational technology, and gender issues.

Prisca Martens is a recent Ph.D. graduate in reading, early literacy, and children's literature and is an Adjunct Professor at the University of Arizona. She previously taught in grades K–3 and is interested in continuing to research and write in the areas of reading and literacy.

Janelle B. Mathis taught English at the middle and high school levels and completed her Ph.D. degree with a focus in children's and adolescent literature. She has been teaching children's literature to preservice teachers and plans to pursue her interests in the role of literature in the curriculum, teacher education, multicultural and literacy issues, and reader response.

T. Gail Pritchard is a recent Ph.D. graduate of the University of Arizona and is currently an Assistant Professor of Curriculum and Instruction at Ft. Hays State University in Kansas. She previously taught English/Language Arts, Social Studies, and Chapter 1 Reading in the public schools and is interested in literature-based instruction in the middle grades.

Jean S. Schroeder has taught primary and multi-age classes in the Tucson Unified School District and is a doctoral student with a major in children's literature. She is on the Editorial Board for the Children's Book Column of *The Reading Teacher.*

Elaine G. Schwartz is currently a doctoral student with a focus in children's literature. Her interests in language and literacy, children's literature, and multicultural education flow directly from her previous teaching experiences with students from the diverse cultures of the American Southwest.

Kathy G. Short is an Associate Professor and teaches and researches in the areas of children's literature, curriculum, collaborative learning environments, and teacher and student inquiry. She is coauthor of *Creating Classrooms for Authors* with Jerome Harste and Carolyn Burke (Heinemann, 1988) and *Creating Curriculum* with Carolyn Burke (Heinemann, 1991). She is coeditor of *Talking about Books* with Kathryn Mitchell Pierce (Heinemann, 1990) and *Teachers are Researchers* (International Reading Association, 1993). She is coeditor of the Children's Book Column for *The Reading Teacher* and the new coeditor of *The New Advocate*.

Terri L. Tarkoff is a sixth grade teacher at Entz Elementary in Mesa, Arizona. She recently completed her master's degree and has taught professional growth classes on literature and writing to other educators in her school district.

Acknowledgments

We want to acknowledge the contributions of David Betts, Leslie Kahn, Gloria Kauffman, and Craig Schwery, who worked on our initial bibliography but were unable to continue with the book manuscript. We especially want to thank Michelle Giunta who ran computer searches, copied articles, and tracked down incomplete references. Her ability to handle these details quickly and efficiently kept us going when we could have become overwhelmed with the enormity of this task. We also want to thank the College of Education for a research grant that supported this work and our colleagues in the Department of Language, Reading and Culture for their confidence in our ability to finish this book.

Introduction

The use of children's literature in the curriculum has been receiving a great deal of attention in schools and universities. This interest has established a need to explore the knowledge base that supports the theory, research, and practice related to children's literature. An examination of studies of children's literature, however, reveals only a few recent syntheses of research in this area. Even experts on this topic are unable to identify complete and current syntheses in children's literature. *Research and Professional Resources in Children's Literature* attempts to fill this void by listing and describing recent research and publications. This book pulls together the resources to support teachers, librarians, and researchers in their search for previous studies on a research topic, strategies for using literature in the classroom, or books on a particular topic.

There is a perception among educators that extensive research has not been done in children's literature. Many even question whether children's literature is a scholarly field. However, it is essential for the purposes of research and curriculum development to establish a scholarly base for children's literature as an active field of research. As researchers in schools and universities explore new directions of inquiry, they need access to previous research. Teachers in schools and universities can use this research base to support the development of curricula in their classrooms and to provide evidence to administrators and parents of the base for their curricula.

The authors of this book first came together in a seminar to examine current work in children's literature. Our frustration with the lack of research syntheses was the beginning of our search for the pieces of the patchwork quilt of research on children's literature. To discover what did exist, we conducted hand searches of journals we felt were most likely to contain research on children's literature and ran a number of computer searches. Our work was aided by an annotated bibliography on children's literature research from 1985–1988, compiled by Jane Bingham (1989). We quickly realized that an extensive body of research does exist, but it is difficult to locate because it cuts across many disciplines, including literary criticism, education, library science, psychology, history, women's studies, critical theory, and sociology. The time-consuming nature of searching for references across such diverse fields led us to limit our initial focus to research published between 1988 and 1991.

The final project for the seminar was to prepare an annotated bibliography of research on children's literature from 1988 to 1991—the bibliography we felt should have been available when we began our search. As we read and annotated this research, we were surprised to find that researchers in different fields seemed to lack knowledge about one another's work. Researchers whose major focus was either library science, English education, literary criticism, reading education, or children's literature rarely cited work from other disciplines. This isolation from others conducting research on children's literature was also apparent at professional conferences. Researchers were well informed about their specific areas of interest, but they did not appear to be knowledgeable across the different fields within children's literature. For example, researchers in reading education conducting research on literature discussion rarely cited earlier research on this topic from the field of children's literature. One explanation for this problem, as our experience proved, was the difficulty of locating the research. Each group of researchers seemed to work on its own piece of the quilt without considering and connecting to the other pieces and without a vision of the whole.

Because we had spent so much time identifying and locating the research, we had only just begun to discuss the issues in it when the seminar came to an end. We had had a glimpse of the quilt but had not yet fit the pieces together. When we looked at the wealth of information we had collected, we decided to develop a book summarizing research in the field for educators in schools and universities. We expanded the contents of our original bibliography to make it more useful for classroom teachers, librarians, and university educators as they explore the knowledge base of children's literature and its use in schools. We then decided to annotate the major journals on children's literature and the many professional books now being published to support the use of children's literature in schools and libraries. By stitching all of these pieces together, we believe we have created a patchwork quilt that will give educators a sense of the relationships and connections among work in various disciplines.

Creating this book was a collaborative experience of coming together to discuss major decisions and selection criteria and working in small groups to gather, read, and annotate articles. The tasks were often tedious, and it would have been easy to abandon our commitment to this book if we had not been working together. We were fortunate to have elementary and middle school teachers, doctoral students, and teacher educators from the fields of children's literature, reading, early literacy, library science, literary criticism, and English education as members of our writing team. Our diverse perspectives and knowledge bases were essential to finding and understanding the different quilt pieces and threads of research encountered in this project.

The book is divided into three sections. Section I focuses on children's literature research published from January 1985 through December 1993 and includes a discussion of our procedures for identifying, listing, and annotating that research. The section is divided into major categories by areas of research. Each category begins with an overview of the major issues and trends of the research in that section. The introduction is followed by annotations of research reviews, books, and selected articles, and by lists of other published studies and dissertations.

Section II highlights professional journals that educators can use to locate reviews of children's literature, lists of books on particular topics, articles on using literature in the classroom, and research on children's literature. Annotations and a chart on the contents of these journals will help educators locate the resources that best meet their professional needs and interests. Descriptions of other journals that occasionally carry research on children's literature are also included. This section ends with a complete listing of the journals searched by hand for Section I.

Section III contains annotations of many professional books on children's literature. Books in this section focus on the theoretical foundations of literature in the classroom, literature discussion and response, broad surveys of children's literature, sociopolitical and cultural issues, genre studies, literature in the reading and language arts curriculum, literature across the curriculum, collections of activities and ideas using children's literature, author, illustrator, and poet studies, and bibliographies of children's and adolescent literature.

Each section contains research or professional resources aimed at elementary and middle school contexts, specifically preschool through grade 8 (age 14). Research and resources relevant to high school contexts and the teaching of children's literature in university and college classrooms exist, but they are not included in this book. A review of 25 years of research in young adult literature is currently being conducted, and initial reports from this research are available (Poe, Samuels, & Carter, 1993).

In the process of preparing this book, we noted that the authors of the research had different perspectives on children's literature. Some took a literary perspective and viewed literature as a discipline with its own content and ways of knowing. Others viewed literature as a vehicle for teaching students to read and write or for teaching the content of subject areas such as science and social studies. Still others viewed literature as a means of addressing social, political, and cultural issues. We searched for research, journals, and professional books reflecting each of these perspectives, although we found that most researchers focused on their own perspective without referencing other views.

Our goal was to make this book a valuable resource for educators in schools and universities who want to know more about children's literature. We examined our own needs as teachers, librarians, and researchers, and we tried to pull together the resources that would support our work—whether we were looking for a book to read aloud, a strategy to support discussion, or previous studies on a research topic. During the process of collecting so many diverse pieces of research, we often felt lost in a maze of seemingly different patterns and colors that sometimes appeared unrelated to one another. Gradually, the pieces came together to create a patchwork quilt that gave us a broader picture. We welcome suggestions from readers on other pieces that might be added to this quilt.

References

Bingham, J. (1989). *Research in children's and young adult literature: An annotated bibliography of articles and dissertations, 1985–1988*. Report prepared for the National Council of Teachers of English CLA\ALAN Research in Children's and Young Adult Literature Preconference, Charleston, SC.

Poe, E., Samuels, B., & Carter, B. (1993). Twenty-five years of research in young adult literature: Past perspectives and future directions. *Youth Services in Libraries, 7*(1), 65–73.

Section I: Research on Children's Literature

This section represents the major focus of our work and reflects many hours of gathering and reading articles, browsing university library shelves, running computer searches, and hunting down references. The section begins with an overview describing our search strategies and selection criteria for research articles. This overview is followed by the categories of research and lists of studies.

Search Strategies for Locating Research

Computer searches of various databases and hand searches of selected journals were conducted to locate research studies. Based on the preparation of our original bibliography, we knew that computer searches were inadequate in identifying research on children's literature. One of the difficulties with computer searches is that the descriptors used by particular databases often are not specific or up to date enough to reflect current trends in the field. Articles we located through hand searches often did not appear under the correct descriptors, which led us to question the procedures and background knowledge of the personnel who entered the studies into the databases. Another major problem was that articles were identified as research only if they were included in research journals, so many studies involving teacher research and many content analyses were not identified as research. Consequently, the majority of studies included in this book were located through hand searches, and computer searches were used to identify articles from other journals and as a check on our hand searches.

We created a list of journals that contained research on children's literature by using the Bingham bibliography (1989) and several research reviews from sources such as Hearne (1988) and *The Handbook of Research on Teaching the English Language Arts* (Flood, et al., 1991). We also added other journals familiar to us from our own professional reading. A hand search of 74 journals for 1988–1991 was conducted to determine whether they included research on children's literature. Based on this search, the number of journals for review was reduced to 43. A complete listing of the 43 journals that were searched for January 1985 through December 1993 is contained in Section III.

Computer searches in the ERIC system were conducted for educational articles published between 1985 and 1993 using the following descriptors: poetry, reading aloud to others, reading interests, recreational reading, storytelling, literary devices, nursery rhymes, picture books, reader response, children's literature, and content analysis. Additional searches were run using cultural differences and children's literature, cultural differences and reader response, crosscultural studies and children's literature, crosscultural studies and reader response, crosscultural studies and adolescents, and reader response and _____ (specific ethnic groups such as Native American or Hispanic). A search was conducted using children's literature and research as the descriptors, but this search located only a few of the existing articles. We checked the *Social Science Index* and *Abstracts of the Modern Language Association* under children's literature and did the same searches for dissertation abstracts.

In addition to searching for individual research studies, we looked for reviews of research on children's literature. The reviews and individual studies were examined for references that had not been located previously by either the hand or computer searches.

We wanted the research we described to be easily accessible to educators in any community through their own libraries and interlibrary loan or through direct contact with specific journals. Consequently, ERIC documents that have not been published as journal articles are not included because of the difficulty many readers might have in obtaining these documents. Dissertations are listed due to their availability through University Microfilms and interlibrary loan.

Reviewing and Organizing the Research

W e collected any article from the hand and computer searches that appeared to be research on children's literature. These articles were then read by group members to determine whether they were actually research on children's literature and to identify the category of research. The categories were established during our initial review of the research from 1988–1991 and through examinination of other research reviews.

The following criteria were used to determine whether an article would be included here:

- conducted with students in preschool through grade 8 (ages 0–14);
- used intact pieces of children's literature; and
- focused on examining some aspect of children's literature or its use.

One of the issues we encountered was how broadly to define "children's literature." In the studies we examined, the researchers frequently used excerpts from books and stories from literature anthologies. After much discussion, we agreed to include studies that relied on stories from anthologies and commercially produced sets of predictable books as long as the complete story was used. In general, research using excerpts from a piece of children's literature is not included unless the researchers preserved a complete unit of meaning in those excerpts. With only a few exceptions, however, the research listed in this review involved trade books and whole pieces of children's literature.

Another issue we faced was whether to include studies of reading comprehension, vocabulary, and word recognition that used children's literature as the reading material but without a focus on the literature itself. Because this research primarily involved studies of reading skills and processes and the researchers' questions did not relate to literature or its use, these studies were excluded from this review. We also excluded responses and rebuttals to specific research studies because we could not consistently locate them, and they did not fit our criteria for selection as actual research studies.

We found that articles included in journals for a broad audience of teachers and teacher educators often did not include the information needed to identify them as research. Articles in research journals were set up with clear formats indicating research questions, methodology, and findings. Articles in journals directed at classroom teachers and teacher educators often did not include discussion of the research methodology but focused on what had occurred. We learned to look for key words at the beginning or end of each article that indicated authors had studied or systematically examined their topics. These key words included *study, investigate, question, examine, results, findings, conclusions, data collection*, and *analysis*. We were able to identify some articles as research only because of our familiarity with the author's work. We were especially concerned about omitting studies by teacher researchers. As we examined the articles, we used Cochran-Smith and Lytle's, (1993) definition of research as systematic, intentional inquiry to determine if an article should be included.

As we read through studies, we met periodically as a group to discuss problems in defining the criteria and to refer articles that were questionable to another reader. Once the studies to be reviewed were determined, we divided into groups of three with each group taking a number of research categories to read and critique. These groups read through all of the articles in their categories and met to discuss the characteristics, trends, and issues within a particular category.

It became clear that, for reasons of space, all of the articles in a particular category could not be annotated in this book. We did want to give readers a good sense of the range of studies within a particular category, and so the decision was made to annotate a representative sample of about 25 percent of the articles in a particular category or subcategory. Occasionally, more than 25 percent were annotated in order to represent the full range of research or because the total number of studies within the category was small. The following criteria were used to choose articles for annotation:

- represents a series of similar studies within the larger category (a particular trend in topics);
- reflects the range of research in terms of topics, methodologies, findings, date of publication, and age levels;
- is cited frequently as seminal or groundbreaking; and
- represents an exceptional study that stands apart from the other studies included in that category.

In order to choose articles for annotation, each group had to decide on major themes and trends within a category or subcategory. The introductions for each category grew out of these decisions. The articles for annotation were chosen based on the characteristics discussed in the introductions, and the remaining articles were then simply listed under each category.

Drafts for each of the categories were submitted to the entire group and revised. The entire document was then reviewed and, based on this review, some studies were moved to different categories. Our definitions of the particular categories were continually discussed and refined.

The research on children's literature included in this book is divided into categories and subcategories as shown on the contents page. The introduction for each category begins with a definition of the category and a discussion of major trends in the topics and issues specific to that category. Other characteristics are identified such as the age levels studied, the contexts within which the research was conducted, and the types of research methods used. The introductions also indicate who is doing this type of research and the journals where this research is typically published. Categories with a large number and range of studies were divided into subcategories. These subcategories are also defined and discussed. Suggestions and recommendations for further research complete the introductions.

If research reviews or books were located for a category or subcategory, these sources are annotated immediately after the introduction. The selected articles are then annotated, and a list of additional articles, chapters, and dissertations follows. Studies published prior to 1985 are occasionally included if they were frequently cited in the more recent research. Studies included in the yearbooks of the National Reading Conference are included as articles, not book chapters, because of the nature of these yearbooks.

There may be studies that have been omitted or articles that are included that are reflective essays rather than research. Our decisions about what to include and our comments in the introductions are based on careful and systematic reading and analysis of a large body of research but also reflect our own beliefs and experiences as educators. We invite readers to send us their comments about our statements as well as additional references which may have eluded us.

Trends and Issues in Children's Literature Research

Although each category includes a discussion of the trends and issues for a particular type of research, there are trends and issues that run across the different categories. The two largest categories of research are Thematic Content Analysis and Reader Response Research. Family and Preschool Literacy, Literature-Based Classrooms, and Instructional Strategies also had large numbers of studies. Two areas where little research currently exists are technology and the use of literature in content area learning and inquiry.

There is a definite trend toward more qualitative research methodologies. Many of the content analyses of literature now use qualitative methods to critically examine issues within a broader context instead of simply counting the number of occurrences of a particular element. The research on children's use of literature in schools is moving toward long-term studies conducted within the actual context of ongoing classroom life instead of pulling children out of the classroom to complete research tasks. This trend is especially evident in reader response research, descriptive studies of literature-based classrooms, and research on teachers' beliefs and practices. The research conducted within classrooms creates new knowledge for the field but also appears to have a beneficial effect for the teachers, students, and administrators participating in the study. However, certain categories, such as research on reading attitudes and interests, still primarily use experimental methodologies that involve little or no actual observation of children.

While the majority of research is conducted by university educators, many more teachers are engaging in and reporting research from their own classrooms. In many studies, teachers have moved from the role of subjects of research to informants for and collaborators with university researchers. Students are still primarily viewed as subjects and occasionally as informants. Particularly in reader response research, students have a greater voice in the research and, in a few studies, were viewed as collaborators and researchers. Authors and illustrators are also becoming researchers who critically analyze their own work instead of that work serving only as the subject of literary analyses by university researchers.

As stated earlier, researchers in the fields of library science, literary criticism, and education tend to cite only those in their own field, to stay within particular categories, and to publish in separate journals. The isolation and lack of communication among these fields and between educators in children's literature and reading continues to be evident. Researchers from the field of literary criticism primarily examine texts separate from any reader other than themselves. Library science researchers primarily conduct content analyses of texts. They also examine readers but through circulation records and surveys rather than through actual observation and interaction. Researchers in education focus on classrooms and rarely reference the critical sociopolitical issues raised in the work of researchers from library science and literary criticism. Each of these fields has a great deal to learn from the others, both in terms of the content of their studies and of exploring other research methodologies. Taxel (1989) suggests one way this might occur is by bringing together content analyses of social issues in children's literature with reader response research.

In terms of studies in classrooms, further research in all categories is needed with middle school students, bilingual students, and students representing a broader diversity of cultures and learning needs. To date, most of the research focuses on children in grades 3–6 (ages 9–12). The research on preschool children primarily consists of studies that demonstrate that if adults read aloud to young children, the children will become successful readers. This research needs to move on to a wider range of issues related to literature and young children.

Working through this review and analysis of the research on children's literature has broadened our perspectives of what we consider research. We were excited to find a large body of research on children's literature from so many different perspectives and disciplines. Many of these studies offered new insights into children's literature and curricula. Within each category, we also saw possibilities for further research and were energized by those possibilities. We hope that readers will find their own possibilities by examining this review of research and piecing together their own patchwork quilt to create a broader view of the field of children's literature.

References

Bingham, J. (1989). *Research in children's and young adult literature: An annotated bibliography of articles and dissertations, 1985–1988.* Report prepared for the National Council of Teachers of English CLA\ALAN Research in Children's and Young Adult Literature Preconference, Charleston, SC.

Cochran-Smith, M., & Lytle, S. (1993). *Inside/outside: Teachers, research, and knowledge.* New York: Teachers College Press.

Flood, J., Jensen, J., Lapp, D., & Squire, J. (Eds.). (1991). *Handbook of research on teaching the English language arts.* New York: Macmillan.

Hearne, B. (1988). Problems and possibilities: U.S. research in children's literature. *School Library Journal, 43*(11), 27–31.

Taxel, J. (1989). Children's literature: A research proposal from the perspective of the sociology of school knowledge. *Language, authority and criticism: Readings on the school textbook* (pp. 32–45). New York: Falmer.

Theoretical Analysis

Theoretical analysis is the examination of the theoretical underpinnings of the text or the transaction between reader and text. These underpinnings may include literary theory, learning theory, developmental theory, or any of the theories nested within these, such as feminist or Marxist interpretations. Because every article is written from a theoretical perspective, theoretical analyses support readers in identifying the point of view reflected in a particular article. Theoretical analyses are also the foundation for developing new theories about children's literature and its use with children in classrooms.

The studies in this section range from the purely theoretical to an essay with a base in developmental theory. Among these studies are reviews of recent theoretical positions regarding literature's role in reading development and the political stance of new theoretical and critical approaches to the criticism of children's literature. Other articles develop theory related to play and children's literature, the relationship between oral traditions and written stories, distinctions between adult culture and the culture of childhood, the value of literature in itself as opposed to its use with children, and models of response to literature. The studies in this category cover a wide range of topics and do not fit into particular subcategories. The majority of authors in this section are university professors in the fields of literary theory and criticism or education. The articles primarily appeared in journals of literary criticism.

Given the range of the few studies in this category, it is difficult to note trends or make suggestions for further research. We are concerned that more theoretical studies were not located. Distinguishing theoretical research from reflective essays was difficult, and we have probably over-looked theoretical studies that should have been included. We also realize that literary theorists have primarily focused on adult literature, with the assumption that children's literature is either a substandard form of literature that does not need a theory or a miniature version of adult literature to which current literary theories can be applied. The development of literary criticism focusing on children's literature needs to be further addressed by theorists.

Reviews of Research

Sawyer, W. (1987). Literature and literacy: A review of research. *Language Arts, 64*(1), 33–39.

> This review of research summarizes the major theoretical positions on the connection between literature and reading development, empirical studies on this connection, and issues based on this research. It particularly focuses on the study and theory of narrative and story.

Zipes, J. (1990). Taking political stock: New theoretical and critical approaches to Anglo-American children's literature in the 1980's. *The Lion and the Unicorn, 14*(1), 7–22.

> Zipes argues that there has been an ideological shift in the criticism of children's books from bland literary histories to studies exploring the sociological, historical, and political aspects of children's literature. Reviews of the major theorists who emphasize the political aspects of literary criticism demonstrate the shift to a concern for the ideological impact of literature on young readers and their socialization.

Articles with Annotations

Armstrong, K. (1992). Dynamics of change: Speculation on a forthcoming model of response to literature. In C.K. Kinzer & D.J. Leu (Eds.), *Literacy research, theory, and practice: Views from many perspectives* (41st yearbook of the

National Reading Conference, pp. 275–281). Chicago, IL: National Reading Conference.

> Armstrong describes the three previous metaphors for the reading process—the mechanistic or text based, the sociopolitical or reader based, and the organic or response based—and proposes instead the holonomic metaphor. Basing her holonomy model on theoretical physics, she proposes that the organization of reading is holographic in the sense that it is a whole and all the parts contain all the elements of the whole, thus blurring the distinctions between reader and writer and moving a step beyond Rosenblatt's transactional theory (see p. 198). The other metaphors she regards as nesting within the holonomic theory.

Nodelman, P. (1992). The other: Orientalism, colonialism, and children's literature. *Children's Literature Association Quarterly, 17*(1), 29–35.

> Nodelman looks at children's literature from a cultural perspective and views children as an oppressed cultural group that is misinterpreted by its oppressors—adults. Edward Said's investigation of European attitudes toward Orientalism is used as a template to develop 16 parallel points between Said's descriptions and current representations of childhood in both child psychology and children's literature. Nodelman views children's literature from this perspective as an instrument of adult imperialism.

Additional Articles

Crago, H. (1993). Why readers read what writers write. *Children's Literature in Education, 24*(4), 277–289.

Dressman, M. (1993). Lionizing lone wolves: The cultural romantics of literacy workshops. *Curriculum Inquiry, 23*(3), 245–263.

Ewers, H.H. (1992). Children's literature and the traditional art of storytelling. *Poetics Today, 13*(1), 169–178.

Hade, D. (1994). Aiding and abetting the basalization of children's literature. *The New Advocate, 7*(1), 29–44.

Sarland, C. (1985). Piaget, Blyton, and story: Children's play and the reading process. *Children's Literature in Education, 16*(2), 102–109.

Dissertations

Darlington, S.F. (1990). *Literature as visual response and aesthetic experience: An alternative approach*. Unpublished doctoral dissertation, Iowa State University, Ames. (*Dissertation Abstracts International–A*, 51/12, p. 4005)

Eberdt, K.A. (1990). *Research conceptions of adult and college reader response to literature*. Unpublished doctoral dissertation, University of British Columbia, Vancouver.

Lastinger, V.C. (1989). *Littérature féminine et écriture enfantine: Quelques implications de la critique féministe*. Unpublished doctoral dissertation, University of Georgia, Athens. (*Dissertation Abstracts International–A*, 50/09, p. 2919)

Leith, R.M. (1993). *The voice of the book and the voice of the child: Whole language as poststructuralist literary theory*. Unpublished doctoral dissertation, University of Arizona, Tucson.

Sullivan, D.L. (1988). *A rhetoric of children's literature as epideictic discourse*. Unpublished doctoral dissertation, Rensselaer Polytechnic Institute, Troy, New York. (*Dissertation Abstracts International–A*, 49/11, p. 3204)

Thematic Content Analysis

Thematic content analysis is the use of a theory or theme to analyze a text or series of texts. The theory or theme is used as an analytical device, the main focus being analysis of the text rather than development of theory. In this form of content analysis, the literary work is evaluated according to a particular theoretical, political, sociological, or psychological framework. Researchers undertake content analyses for a variety of reasons. Some make connections across themes or genres, while others focus on insights gained through diverse perspectives such as narrative theory, semiotics, critical theory, or feminist pedagogy.

The primary methodology used in the majority of this research is qualitative. These studies provide in-depth contextual analyses and so present a powerful exploration of content within the framework of complete texts. A few researchers use a quantitative approach in which content items, counted out of context, are analyzed in terms of number of occurrences. These quantitative studies offer less insight for readers than qualitative studies due to their lack of critical analysis. In both methodologies, the key to content analysis is the development of specific criteria for interpretation and analysis. Sometimes those criteria are developed prior to the study from a review of previous research, and other times the criteria emerge from the data, the actual books being analyzed.

In identifying articles for this category, it was often difficult to distinguish between reflective essays examining the content of children's literature and content analysis. The length of typical journal articles often does not allow for a full description and development of the analytical framework. We looked for evidence that authors were working from a theory or point of view that was then used to examine literature.

The majority of content analyses are by university professors from the fields of literary criticism and education. A few contributions from graduate students, classroom teachers, and librarians are also present in the body of work reviewed. For the most part, articles containing strict content analyses are located in literary criticism journals. Pedagogical suggestions based on content analyses are integral to articles that appear in education journals.

The content analyses we located focused on a variety of genres from picture books to novels and a range of issues related to many different aspects of life. Four general subcategories of issues were developed from our examination of these content analyses: Culture, Social Issues, Life Cycles, and Gender. These subcategories overlap, and some studies might be placed in more than one. Our choice of subcategory reflected the major focus of the content analysis.

The broad subcategory of Culture encompasses the material aspects and the nonmaterial values, beliefs, and traditions of human society. Research studies within this subcategory focus on topics such as cultural diversity, cultural identity, cultural perspectives, minority and ethnic groups, acculturation, and crosscultural issues. A number of these studies examine the availability and accuracy of books about particular cultural experiences, while another group of studies focuses on the ways in which books portray the experiences of people representing several distinct cultures.

The subcategory of Social Issues focuses on social problems caused by the economic, political, and social inequities of modern Western civilization. Research studies within this subcategory address the causal relationships among power relations and social class, ethnicity, race, minority status, gender, and modern technology. These issues are addressed within specific social and historical contexts. The tone of many of these articles indicates that they are intended to raise the reader's social consciousness and provide visions of positive social change. Specific research studies within this subcategory cover such topics as homelessness, racism, social and political movements, censorship, environmental degradation, utopian visions, and the social significance of technology.

The many stages of human life constitute the basis of the subcategory of Life Cycles. Content analyses in this subcategory touch upon family, death and dying, adolescence, coming of age, and the elderly. Themes and issues related to growing up, work, pain, and suffering are prominent in this subcategory. Several studies point out differences between adults' and children's perspectives on the issues that are important to children as they grow physically and socially.

Gender refers to the socially constructed roles ascribed to males and females in every society. The content analyses in this subcategory cross time and space to cover sexism, socialization, role models, gender equity, power, feminist perspectives within texts, and feminist content analyses. A number of these articles examine gender issues within specific ethnic groups. A large group of these studies involve a reassessment of books and authors from past eras.

Future research would profit from attending to issues of both content and methodology. We believe that qualitative studies, particularly those that offer pedagogical implications, could facilitate critical responses and discussion of the literature among educators. They provide contextually based insights, demonstrate the use of literature as the basis for pedagogy, and ultimately open the door to critical thinking and the development of democratic classrooms. Quantitative studies that count content items offer very little critical analysis and seem to have limited value for educators.

Qualitative researchers who are currently publishing in literary criticism journals should be encouraged also to publish in education journals where their work can inform educators in the selection and evaluation of literature. As has been mentioned before, there is currently little overlap among researchers publishing in the fields of literary criticism, library science, and education. These fields do not appear to inform or build upon one another's insights.

The diverse array of modern children's literature focusing on global issues provides ample opportunity for further in-depth analyses of the relationships between children's literature and multiculturalism, environmental degradation, and issues of social justice and human rights. We would like to see content analyses that span a wide range of topics, such as family and life cycles, gender, social issues, crosscultural concerns, environmental issues, and other current and timely topics. In addition, we hope to see more studies that demonstrate the vital connections between literature and issues critical to students' lives. Research on these topics would aid teachers in broadening students' opportunities to envision other realities and to become active and responsible citizens. Ultimately, these studies will be judged by their social relevance within the context of an increasingly complex and many-cultured world.

Culture

Book

Sims, R. (1982). *Shadow & substance: Afro-American experience in contemporary children's fiction*. Urbana, IL: National Council of Teachers of English.

> This monograph reports on a survey and content analysis of 150 children's books of contemporary realistic fiction about African Americans published between 1965 and

1979. The books fell into four major categories: (1) realistic fiction with a social conscience; (2) melting pot books; (3) culturally conscious fiction; and (4) the image-makers. These categories are used frequently in later research on the depiction of African Americans and other ethnic groups in children's literature.

Reviews of Research

Harris, V. (1991). Multicultural curriculum: African American children's literature. *Young Children, 46*(2), 37–44.

The author uses this review of research to provide a historical and cultural perspective on African American children's literature. She addresses the issues of a definition of African American literature as culturally conscious, the history and status of the literature, and the major authors and their philosophies. The review ends with implications for early childhood education.

Reimer, K.M. (1992). Multiethnic literature: Holding fast to dreams. *Language Arts, 69*(1), 14–21.

This review examines content analysis research on the representation of African Americans, Hispanic Americans, Asian Americans, and Native Americans in children's literature. The author also includes results from her own survey of books on recommended reading lists. Based on this review, issues related to the writing and publishing of multiethnic literature are raised.

Ross, E. (1991). Children's books on contemporary North American Indian/native/metis life: A selected bibliography of books and professional reading materials. *Canadian Children's Literature*, (61), 29–43.

This review examines research on racism and bias toward Native Americans in Canadian children's literature and professional books. The author presents a number of studies of criteria for evaluating stereotypes and includes a bibliography of recommended books and materials based on these criteria.

Articles with Annotations

Cai, M. (1992). A balanced view of acculturation: Comments on Lawrence Yep's three novels. *Children's Literature in Education*, *23*(2), 107–118.

> Three of Yep's novels, *The Star Fisher, Dragonwings,* and *Child of the Owl,* are discussed as books that contain positive images of Chinese Americans. The process of acculturation can be examined through analyzing the fundamental problems that Yep presents in his portrayals of Chinese American experiences.

Maher, S.N. (1992). Encountering others: The meeting of cultures in Scott O'Dell's *Island of the Blue Dolphins* and *Sing Down the Moon. Children's Literature in Education*, *23*(4), 215–227.

> This content analysis focuses on Scott O'Dell's "counter-westerns" in which he gives voice to the oppressed through a strong female character. The characters of Karana in *Island of the Blue Dolphins* and Bright Morning in *Sing Down the Moon* represent O'Dell's exploration of native cultures and the need to present history from different perspectives.

Rahn, S. (1987). Early images of American minorities: Rediscovering Florence Crannell Means. *The Lion and the Unicorn*, *11*(1), 98–115.

> This study explores the works of Florence Crannell Means, whose novels about minority groups such as American Indians, African Americans, migrant workers, and Japanese Americans were published in the 1930s and 1940s. Means's position, as a white author writing about minority groups, was controversial during this period and remains controversial today.

Russell, D.L. (1990). Cultural identity and individual triumph in Virginia Hamilton's *M.C. Higgins, the Great. Children's Literature in Education*, *21*(4), 253–259.

> Through content analysis, Russell examines Virginia Hamilton's use of symbolism of the African American

experience in *M.C. Higgins, the Great*. Specifically, the study focuses on how the African American hero survives through coming to terms with the importance of cultural heritage and understanding the signficance of community.

Additional Articles

Bubules, N.C. (1986). Tootle: A parable of schooling and destiny. *Harvard Educational Review, 56*(3), 239–256.

Cai, M. (1993). Folks, friends and foes: Relationships between humans and animals in some Eastern and Western folktales. *Children's Literature in Education*, 24(2), 73–83.

Chamberlain, K. (1992). The Bobsey Twins hit the trail: Or, out West with children's series fiction. *Children's Literature Association Quarterly, 17*(1), 9–15.

Cornell, C.E. (1993). Language and culture monsters that lurk in our traditional rhymes and folktales. *Young Children, 48*(6), 40–46.

Iskander, S.P. (1993). Arabic adventures and American investigators: Cultural values in adolescent detective fiction. *Children's Literature, 21*, 118–131.

Miller, J., & Schlessinger, J.H. (1988). Trends in the portrayal of minorities in the Nancy Drew series. *Journal of Youth Services in Libraries, 1*(3), 329–333.

Miller, M.Y. (1987). In days of old: The middle ages in children's non-fiction. *Children's Literature Association Quarterly, 12*(4), 167–171.

Shannon, G. (1988). Making a home of one's own: The young in cross-cultural fiction. *English Journal, 77*(5), 14–19.

Shavit, Z. (1992). Literary interference between German and Jewish-Hebrew children's literature during the enlightment: The case of Campe. *Poetics Today, 13*(1), 41–61.

Torsney, C.B. (1992). The politics of low and high culture: Representations of music in some recent children's picture books. *The Lion and the Unicorn, 16*(2), 176–183.

Dissertations

Burgess, V.A. (1990). *Portrayal of Alaskan Native Americans in children's literature.* Unpublished doctoral dissertation, University of South Carolina, Columbia. (*Dissertation Abstracts International*–A, 51/08, p. 2742)

Carruth, L.P. (1988). *A comparison of contemporary East and West German children's literature on three themes.* Unpublished doctoral dissertation, University of Utah, Provo. (*Dissertation Abstracts International*–A, 49/09, p. 2673)

White, D.R. (1991). *The Mabinogi in children's literature: Welsh legends in English-language children's books.* Unpublished doctoral dissertation, University of Minnesota, Minneapolis. (*Dissertation Abstracts International*–A, 52/08, p. 2938)

Yandell, C.E. (1990). *Spiritual values identified by children's librarians and elementary school children in Newbery Medal and Honor books.* Unpublished doctoral dissertation, University of Arkansas, Fayetteville. (*Dissertation Abstracts International*–A, 51/11, p. 3632)

Social Issues

Articles with Annotations

Bigelow, W. (1992). Once upon a genocide: Christopher Columbus in children's literature. *Language Arts, 69*(2), 111–120.

> Bigelow compares and analyzes the congruence of eight children's books with the historical record and discusses instructional implications. He examines the portrayal of Columbus's character, the portrayal of Native Americans as nonhumans, the justification for cultural genocide, and current understandings of Columbus's legacy.

Geertz-Hyman, T. (1993). Messages about technology in children's literature. *The New Advocate, 6*(2), 123–136.

> This is an exploration of perspectives on technology in a diverse selection of children's literature. Geertz-Hyman found that many authors celebrate technology, while very few question either its environmental or its social impact. The author also discusses a number of books that make a difference by questioning technology and including suggestions for classroom use.

Greenway, B. (1993). "Creeping like a snail unwillingly to school": Negative images of school in children's literature. *The New Advocate, 6*(2), 105–114.

> Greenway's analysis of the image of school in a variety of picture and chapter books leads to a number of important conclusions. Children, as portrayed in literature and in real life, understand the basic messages of social control that are often characteristic of modern schooling: submission to authority and disempowerment. The researcher believes that children's books may provide a meaningful basis for discussion of this issue and perhaps create alternative visions of schooling.

Kohl, H. (1991). The politics of children's literature: The story of Rosa Parks and the Montgomery bus boycott. *Journal of Education, 193*(1), 35–50.

Kohl examines the erroneous implications about Rosa Parks and the Montgomery bus boycott in textbooks and children's books. The author deconstructs numerous myths, including the central myth that Parks was simply a poor, tired seamstress. In reality, Rosa Parks had already gained a place, with other seekers of justice, in the struggle against the Jim Crow laws.

Phillips, A. (1992). "Home itself put into song": Music as metaphorical community. *The Lion and the Unicorn, 16*(2), 145–157.

The focus of this content analysis is on the value of community and how music is used within children's literature to affirm this value. Several books and series are examined to argue that authors create harmonious, nurturing communities in literature through musical metaphors and they use silence to signify isolation. The focus on community is viewed as a response to the social, economic, cultural, and demographic changes caused by industrialization and urbanization.

Shannon, P. (1986). Hidden within the pages: A study of social perspective in young children's favorite books. *The Reading Teacher, 39*(7), 656–663.

In this study, a random sample of 30 books selected as Children's Choices (a project cosponsored by the International Reading Association and the Children's Book Council) from 1978, 1980, and 1982 were examined by three readers to discover if they presented an individualist, collectivist, or balanced social perspective. Results indicated that 29 books represented an individualist perspective, 1 a balanced perspective, and none a collectivist theme.

Additional Articles

Apseloff, M.F. (1992). Abandonment: The new realism of the eighties. *Children's Literature in Education, 23*(2), 101–105.

Bogert, E. (1985). Censorship and "The Lottery." *English Journal, 74*(1), 45–47.

Carey-Webb, A. (1993). Racism and *Huckleberry Finn*: Censorship, dialogue, and change. *English Journal*, *82*(7), 22–34.

Cullingford, C. (1993). "The Right Stuff": The boys' stories of Percy F. Westerman. *Children's Literature in Education*, *24*(1), 53–71.

Gardner, S. (1991). My first rhetoric of domination: The Columbian encounter in children's biographies. *Children's Literature in Education*, 22(4), 275–289.

Gooderham, D. (1993). Still catching them young?: The moral dimension in children's books. *Children's Literature in Education*, *24*(2), 115–121.

Harris, V. (1989). Race consciousness, refinement, and radicalism: Socialization in *The Brownies' Book*. *Children's Literature Association Quarterly*, *14*(4), 192–196.

Harris, V. (1990). From Little Black Sambo to Popo and Fifina: Arna Bontemps and the creation of African–American children's literature. *The Lion and the Unicorn*, *14*(1), 108–127.

Johannessen, L.R. (1993). Young-adult literature and the Vietnam War. *English Journal*, *82*(5), 43–49.

Kellogg, J.L. (1993). The dynamics of dumbing: The case of Merlin. *The Lion and the Unicorn*, 17, 57–72.

Kirk, K.A., & Karbon, J. (1986). Environmental content in award winning children's literature: 1960 through 1982. *Journal of Environmental Education*, *17*(3), 1–7.

Knafle, J.D., Escott, A.L., & Pascarella, E.T. (1988). Assessing values in children's books. *Reading Improvement*, *25*(1), 71–81.

Krips, V. (1993). A notable irrelevance: Class and children's fiction. *The Lion and the Unicorn, 17*(2), 195–209.

Lester, N. (1993). "Alabama Angels" descending into the past. *The Lion and the Unicorn, 17*(2), 210–214.

Logan, M. (1991). Henty and Ashantis. *Children's Literature Association Quarterly, 16*(2), 82–86.

Phillips, J. (1993). The Mem Sahib, the worthy, the rajah and his minions: Some reflections on the class politics of *The Secret Garden. The Lion and the Unicorn, 17*(2), 168–194.

Russell, D. (1993). *The Gammage Cup* as utopian literature for children. *Children's Literature in Education, 24*(4), 241–249.

Stott, J.C., & Francis, C.D. (1993). "Home" and "not home" in children's stories: Getting there and being worth it. *Children's Literature in Education, 24*(3), 158–166.

Tager, F. (1992). A radical culture for children of the working class: *The Young Socialists' Magazine*, 1908–1920. *Curriculum Inquiry, 22*(3), 271–290.

Walter, V.A. (1992). Hansel and Gretel as abandoned children: Timeless images for a postmodern age. *Children's Literature in Education, 23*(4), 203–213.

Wytenbroek, J.R. (1992). The child as creator in McCaffrey's *Dragonsong and Dragonsinger. The Lion and the Unicorn, 16*, 210–214.

Dissertations

Arthur, J. (1991). *Hardly boys: An analysis of behaviors, social changes and class awareness hidden in old text of 'The Hardy Boys Stories,' 1927–1991.* Unpublished doctoral dissertation, Ohio State University, Columbus. (*Dissertation Abstracts International*–A, 52/08, p. 2963)

Devlin, J.T. (1991). *The Caldecott books: Values and visions*. Unpublished doctoral dissertation, Southern Illinois University, Carbondale. (*Dissertation Abstracts International*–A, 53/05, p. 1517)

Harrison, B. (1988). *Moral intensity and heroic possibility in the postwar children's novel*. Unpublished doctoral dissertation, Tufts University, Medford, MA. (*Dissertation Abstracts International*–A, 49/11, p. 3360)

Huang, J. (1989). *A study of prosocial behavior in selected Chinese children's literature*. Unpublished doctoral dissertation, University of Oregon, Eugene. (*Dissertation Abstracts International*–A, 50/11, p. 3503)

Karnes-Duggan, M. (1991). *An analysis of economic values in selected children's literature, 1974–1987*. Unpublished doctoral dissertation, Saint Louis University, MO. (*Dissertation Abstracts International*–A, 52/05, p. 1662)

MacCann, D.C. (1988). *The white supremacy myth in juvenile books about blacks, 1830–1900*. Unpublished doctoral dissertation, University of Iowa, Ames. (*Dissertation Abstracts International*–A, 50/04, p. 1055)

Schulz, A.R. (1987). *A content analysis of the developmental bibliotherapeutic implications of the books nominated for the California Young Reader Medal*. Unpublished doctoral dissertation, University of the Pacific, Stockton, CA. (*Dissertation Abstracts International*–A, 49/10, p. 2918)

Life Cycles

Articles with Annotations

Bat-Ami, M. (1992). The worm song. *Children's Literature Association Quarterly, 17*(4), 31–36.

> This content analysis looks at stories, poems, and songs that use nonhuman characters such as worms and slugs to provide a safe forum for children to explore pain, suffering, and fear. The author is concerned about the lack of respect and dignity toward animals in this literature and argues that children also need to be presented with literature portraying the beautiful and compassionate side of nature.

Burgan, M. (1988). The question of work: Adolescent literature and the Eriksonian paradigm. *Children's Literature in Education, 19*(4), 187–198.

> The question of work—(or "What do you want to be when you grow up?")— is one of the most significant asked in adolescent literature. The author uses Erik Erikson's paradigm of the psychosocial stages of development to analyze many aspects of the concept of work in adolescent literature.

Hartvigsen, M.K., & Hartvigsen, C.B. (1985). Haven Peck's legacy in *A Day No Pigs Would Die*. *English Journal, 74*(4), 41–45.

> The researchers explore how the father in Robert Newton Peck's *A Day No Pigs Would Die* prepares his son for the "beauty and harshness" of life as he is initiated into adulthood. The importance of hard work is continually emphasized. The book comes full circle in the cycle of life, beginning with the birth of a calf and ending with the death of the father.

Harvey, C., & Dowd, F.S. (1993). Death and dying in young adult fiction. *Journal of Youth Services in Libraries, 6*(2), 141–154.

The treatment of death and dying in 25 titles of young adult literature is examined in this content analysis. Instruments were developed to determine whether the stages of dying, the stages of grief, the grief experience, and the coping strategies are portrayed realistically. The main character who dies in each story is analyzed in terms of age, sex, ethnicity, cause of death, and relationship to the other characters.

Morgan, A.L. (1985) The child alone: Children's stories reminiscent of *E.T.: The Extra-Terrestrial. Children's Literature in Education, 16*(3), 131–142.

The focus of this content analysis is on the motif of isolation of the protagonist from home in children's fiction. This motif is related to children's fear of being deserted and of moving from dependence on to independence from their caretakers. The author found four major structural variations to this motif and provides examples of literature for each variation as well as comparing them with one another and with the film *E.T.:The Extra-Terrestrial.*

Vogel, M., & Creadick, A. (1993). Family values and the new adolescent novel. *English Journal, 82*(5), 37–42.

Widespread changes are taking place in family structures and values, and the authors believe literature can help readers cope with and better understand the complex forces at work. They analyzed several young adult novels to see how young people establish an individual identity and find a place for themselves in a larger community. What they found significant in these novels is the power adolescents gain through their experiences.

Additional Articles

Almerico, G.M., & Fillmer, T. (1988). Portrayal of older characters in children's magazines. *Educational Gerontology, 14*(1), 15–31.

Apseloff, M.F. (1991). Death in adolescent literature: Suicide. *Children's Literature Association Quarterly, 16*(1), 234–238.

Berry, J. (1993). Discipline and (dis)order: Paternal socialization in Jacob Abbott's Rollo books. *Children's Literature Association Quarterly, 8*(3), 100–105.

Bosmajian, H. (1985). *Charlie and the Chocolate Factory* and other excremental visions. *The Lion and the Unicorn, 9*, 36–49.

Davis, G.L. (1986). A content analysis of fifty-seven children's books with death themes. *Child Study Journal, 16*(1), 39–54.

Hartvigsen, M.K., & Hartvigsen, C.B. (1987). "Rough and soft, both at once": Winnie Foster's initiation in *Tuck Everlasting. Children's Literature in Education, 18*(3), 176–183.

Kazemek, F.E., & Rigg, P. (1988). There's more to an old person than appears. *Journal of Youth Services in Libraries, 1*(4), 396–406.

Krips, V. (1993). Mistaken identity: Russell Hoban's *Mouse and His Child. Children's Literature, 21*, 92–100.

Mills, C. (1988). The image of work in adolescent fiction. *Journal of Youth Services in Libraries, 2*(1), 76–83.

Moore, R.C. (1993). Boarding school books: A unique literary opportunity. *Journal of Youth Services in Libraries, 6*(4), 378–386.

Moore, T.E., & Mae, R. (1987). Who dies and who cries: Death and bereavement in children's literature. *Journal of Communication, 37*(4), 52–64.

Pouliot, S. (1993, Summer). Les images de la vieillesse dans les albums de jeunesse. *Canadian Children's Literature*, (70), 34–47.

Scott, C. (1992). Between me and the world: Clothes as mediator between self and society in the work of Beatrix Potter. *The Lion and the Unicorn, 16*(2), 192–198.

Sherman, C. (1987). The princess and the wizard: The fantasy worlds of Ursula K. LeGuin and George MacDonald. *Children's Literature Association Quarterly, 12*(1), 24–28.

Thompson, E. (1992). Intergenerational discourse: Collaboration and time travel in Canadian fiction. *Canadian Children's Literature*, (67), 19–31.

Walker, J.M. (1985). *The Lion, the Witch, and the Wardrobe* as rite of passage. *Children's Literature in Education, 16*(3), 177–188.

West, M.I. (1985). Regression and fragmentation of the self in *James and the Giant Peach. Children's Literature in Education, 16*(4), 219–225.

Dissertation

Odoms, L.J. (1992). *A content analysis approach to the depiction of the elderly in literature books for children published between 1950-1966 for grades five through eight.* Unpublished doctoral dissertation, Temple University, Philadelphia, PA. (*Dissertation Abstracts International*–A, 53/05, p. 1393)

Gender

Articles with Annotations

Altmann, A.E. (1992). Welding brass tits on armor: An examination of the quest metaphor in Robin McKinley's *The Hero and the Crown. Children's Literature in Education,* *23*(3), 143–151.

> Altmann uses elements from cognitive anthropologist Victor Turner's theory of liminality and literary analysis to discuss the quest metaphor. She contends that McKinley's text supports the reclamation of the quest metaphor for the female sex. Thus the text provides young readers with a positive example of the heroine in the genre of fantasy.

Kazemek, F.E. (1986). Literature and moral development from a feminine perspective. *Language Arts,* *63*(3), 264–272.

> Kazemek discusses characteristics of a female morality based on the works of Carol Gilligan. He then reviews children's books that he believes exemplify the feminine perspective and provides suggestions for classroom practices that will further children's exploration of morality. These suggestions give full value to Gilligan's notion of a morality of caring based on relationships and connections.

Kissell, S. (1988). "But when at last she really came, I shot her": *Peter Pan* and the drama of gender. *Children's Literature in Education,* *1*(1), 32–40.

> In this feminist analysis, Kissel demonstrates the ways in which Western sex roles are played out to the extreme. In *Peter Pan*, women are infantilized and trivialized; boys escape to female-free Neverneverland. This analysis, based on the feminist works of Dorothy Dinnerstein, Nancy Chodorow, and Susan Griffin, touches on social psychology and the relationship of women to nature.

Mowder, L. (1992). Domestication of desire: Gender, language and landscape in the Little House books. *Children's Literature Association Quarterly, 17*(1), 15–18.

> Mowder situates Laura Ingalls Wilder's Little House books within a broad sociohistorical context. She uses this series to demonstrate parallels between the United States' western expansion, the taming of the wilderness, and the way in which women's socialization led to a silencing of their desires for autonomy and emancipation. This theme is played out throughout the Little House series. Mowder notes that the Little House books were originally intended as a multivolume series for adults.

Nodelman, P. (1992). Males performing in a female space: Music and gender in young adult novels. *The Lion and the Unicorn, 16*(2), 223–239.

> Nodelman's analysis is situated within a broader analytical frame in which femininity is often equated with the private sphere and masculinity with the public sphere. The novelists whose work Nodelman examines use the conventional association of music with gender as a device to define one form of unconventional masculinity, a form separate from the aggressive, "macho" male image. Through the association with music as a separate, female-owned utopian space, unconventional young men come to find their identities.

Stanger, C.A. (1987). *Winnie the Pooh* through a feminist lens. *The Lion and the Unicorn, 11*(2), 34–50.

> Stanger uses male and female feminist criticism in this analysis. She carries her argument beyond the text to the marketing of Pooh, which, she charges, perpetuates patriarchy by reducing the text to simple sign systems of stereotypic images. Stanger concludes that *Winnie the Pooh* presents the vision of an idealized, all-male, presexual, and preliterate world.

Veglahn, N. (1987). Images of evil: Male and female monsters in heroic fantasy. *Children's Literature, 15*, 106–119.

> This researcher discusses an interesting pattern in how male and female authors portray the sex of monsters in

heroic fantasy: men writers depict the worst characteristics of women in their female monsters, and women follow suit in their depiction of male monsters. Differences
in isolation, relationships, emotions, loyalty, and treach-
erousness exemplify images of the opposite sex at its
worst. Veglahn suggests that in the future perhaps both
sexes will merge and that the fascination that monsters
hold for readers may rest in a continuing search for identity.

Zilboorg, C. (1990). *Caddie Woodlawn*: A feminist case
study. *Children's Literature in Education, 23*(2), 109–117.

This article is part of a larger study of feminist main characters in books published from the 1920s through the
1960s. Carol Ryrie Brink's *Caddie Woodlawn*, written in
1935, is one of few novels with a strong female character. This novel serves to exemplify one specific genre of
American novel written by women for young women.

Additional Articles

Agee, J. (1993). Mothers and daughter: Gender-role socialization in two Newbery award books. *Children's Literature
in Education, 24*(3), 165–183.

Anderson, C.C. (1986). Spindle, shuttle, and scissors: Am-
biguous power in the Grimm Brothers' tales. *Children's
Literature in Education, 17*(4), 227–232.

Christian-Smith, L. (1987). Gender, popular culture, and
curriculum: Adolescent romance novels as gender text.
Curriculum Inquiry, 17(4), 365–406.

Davis, M. (1991). Fiction of a feminist: Nellie McClung's
work for children. *Canadian Children's Literature,* (62),
37–51.

Dougherty, W., & Engel, R. (1987). An 80's look for sex
equality in Caldecott winners and Honor books. *The Reading Teacher, 40*(4), 394–398.

Erol, S. (1992). Beyond the divide: Laskey's feminist revision of the westward journey. *Children's Literature Association Quarterly, 17*(1), 5–8.

Fasick, L. (1993). The failure of fatherhood: Maleness and its discontents in Charles Kingsley. *Children's Literature Association Quarterly, 8*(3), 106–111.

Frongia, T. (1993). Merlin's fathers: The sacred and the profane. *Children's Literature Association Quarterly, 8*(3), 120–125.

Hatfield, L. (1993). From master to brother: Shifting the balance of authority in Ursula K. LeGuin's *Farthest Shore* and *Tehanu. Children's Literature, 21,* 43–65.

Keyser, E.L. (1985). Domesticity versus identity: A review of Alcott research. *Children's Literature in Education, 16*(3), 165–175.

Kinman, J., & Henderson, D. (1985). An analysis of sexism in Newbery Medal Award books from 1977 to 1984. *The Reading Teacher, 38*(9), 885–889.

Lastinger, V.D. (1993). Of dolls and girls in nineteenth-century France. *Children's Literature, 21,* 20–42.

Lehnert, G. (1992). The training of the shrew: The socialization and education of young women in children's literature. *Poetics Today, 13*(1), 109–122.

Myers, M. (1986). Impeccable governesses, rational dames, and moral mothers: Mary Wollstonecraft and the female tradition in Georgian children's books. *Children's Literature, 14,* 31–59.

Richardson, A. (1993). Reluctant lords and lame princes: Engendering the male child in nineteenth-century juvenile fiction. *Children's Literature, 21,* 3–19.

Rocha, O.J., & Dowd, F.S. (1993). Are Mexican-American females portrayed realistically in fiction for grades K–3?: A content analysis. *Multicultural Review, 2*(4), 60–70.

Rubio, M. (1992). Subverting the trite: L.M. Montgomery's "room of her own". *Canadian Children's Literature,* (65), 6–39.

Stewig, J. (1988). Fathers: A presence in picture books. *Journal of Youth Services in Libraries, 1*(4), 391–395.

Tarr, C.A. (1992). Fool's gold: Scott O'Dell's formulaic vision of the golden west. *Children's Literature Association Quarterly, 17*(1), 19–23.

Tetenbaum, T., & Pearson, J. (1989). The voices in children's literature: The impact of gender on the moral decisions of storybook characters. *Sex Roles, 20*(7 & 8), 381–395.

Thomas, M. (1992). The discourse of the difficult daughter: A feminist reading of Mary Norton's *Borrowers. Children's Literature in Education, 23*(1), 39–48.

White, H. (1986). Damsels in distress: Dependency themes in fiction for children and adolescents. *Adolescence, 21*(82), 251–256.

Williams, J.A., Jr., Vernon, J.A, Williams, M.C., & Malecha, K. (1987). Sex role socialization in picture books: An update. *Social Science Quarterly, 68*(1), 148–156.

Wolf, V. (1985). Andre Norton: Feminist pied piper in science fiction. *Children's Literature Association Quarterly, 10*(2), 66–70.

Dissertations

Monroe, S.S. (1988). *Images of Native American female protagonists in children's literature, 1928-1988.* Unpublished doctoral dissertation, University of Arizona, Tucson. (*Dissertation Abstracts International*–A, 50/01, p. 89)

Nelson, C.A. (1991). *A content analysis of female and male authors' portrayals of sex roles in science fiction for children from 1970 to 1990*. Unpublished doctoral dissertation, University of Minnesota, Minneapolis. (*Dissertation Abstracts International*–A, 52/01, p. 100)

Vallone, L.M. (1990). *Happiness and virtue: The history and ideology of the novel for girls*. Unpublished doctoral dissertation, State University of New York at Buffalo. (*Dissertation Abstracts International*–A, 51/08, p. 2759)

Text and Literary Analysis

Text and literary analysis examines the characteristics of a text in isolation from a reader other than the researcher. These characteristics may include the origin of a text, such as a translated work; the literary and artistic qualities of the writing or illustrations; or the genre of a book, such as fairy tale or fantasy. This form of content analysis allows researchers and teachers to understand how texts are constructed to offer meaning for readers. A self-contained text can be examined to study a particular literary characteristic or its structural organization. Some researchers see a text as containing specific meanings that are separate from reader and context. Others examine a text as a set of meaning potentials that are transformed in the transaction of reader, text, and context.

There are four major types of studies in this category. The first group examines issues of readability and adaptation in children's books. Some of this research investigates changes in the text or illustrations in cases where literature is adapted for basal readers and there is a subsequent impact on predictability and meaning. A second group analyzes literary or artistic devices used by an author or illustrator. The majority of these studies now focus on illustrations rather than the written text reflecting a major shift in this area of research. One study goes beyond illustration and print to examine the book format and construction. A third group focuses on the use of a literary device across a number of books. The fourth group looks at a selection of texts organized according to structural principles, such as genre and archetype. These studies include the use of a myth-critical approach, which examines the genres of myth and fantasy, and an analysis of the characteristics of translated books.

Most of the authors in this section are university researchers who examine texts in isolation from classrooms and children. Most come from the field of literary criticism, and many have a major focus on children's literature. A few authors come from the fields of library science or education. Because most of these articles were published in journals from the fields of English and literary criticism, the research does not include implications for readers in the classroom and, consequently, has had little impact on teachers. In addition, many of these studies continue to be dominated by a New Criticism point of view, which accepts the perspective that texts have a specific meaning to be transferred to readers. Future research must recognize the complexity of the reading event and consider texts within the transaction of reader, text, and context.

However, a recent trend of studies in this category has the potential to inform educators. This research analyzes illustrations and book formats, the predictability of texts, intertextual connections across literature, and the meaning potential of other sign systems, such as music metaphors in literature. The perspectives of a broader range of researchers, particularly those of teacher educators and classroom teachers, would provide many more possible points of connection from this research to the classroom context.

Articles with Annotations

Alberghene, J.M. (1985). Writing in *Charlotte's Web. Children's Literature in Education, 16*(1), 32–44.

> This study analyzes the role of Charlotte's writing as it affects the reader. Alberghene states that the absence of adult believers in Charlotte's abilities pulls the child into the story because Charlotte's struggles with the craft of writing parallel those of children. The researcher concludes that reading the text welcomes the child into the "community of writers."

Evans, G. (1992). Harps and harpers in contemporary fantasy. *The Lion and the Unicorn, 16*(2), 199–209.

> The literary use of the harp in children's fantasy is traced to identify three motifs: the harp is used to embody the idea of the power of music; skill on the harp is often a test of the special worth of a character; and the harp may itself be the vehicle of redemptive sacrifice. In particular, the harp is used to symbolize the value of music in nature and society.

Goodman, K.S., Maras, L., & Birdseye, D. (1994). Look! Look! Who stole the pictures from the picture book?: The basalization of picture books. *The New Advocate, 7*(1), 1–24.

> This text analysis, conducted by a teacher educator and teacher researchers, focuses on the adaptation of picture books in basal readers. The authors argue that the adaptations take both the drama and story out of the illustrations and change the fundamental nature of picture books to make them fit the basal's physical and instructional constraints, regardless of the effect on the story itself.

Johnson, P. (1992). Children's books as architecture. *Children's Literature in Education, 23*(3), 131–142.

> The author argues that little research has been conducted on the book form itself and that current innovations in three dimensional design and production open a new era in children's books. Johnson examines these books as pieces of architecture—rather than mere gimmicks—that will change how children read and interpret literature.

Nickolajeva, M. (1991). A typological approach to the study of *The Root Cellar. Canadian Children's Literature*, (63), 53–59.

> The researcher applies an intertextual analysis, rather than a simple comparative analysis, to Janet Lunn's *The Root Cellar*. The intertextual technique, first used by Russian critic Mikhail Bakhtin and introduced to the West

by Julia Kristeva is used to show that the fantasy genre is capable of producing new and original text.

Steig, M. (1993). The importance of the visual text in *Architecture of the Moon*: Mothers, teapots, et al. *Canadian Children's Literature*, (70), 22–33.

In this literary analysis, the researcher examines Tim Wynne-Jones and Ian Wallace's *Architect of the Moon*. Steig argues that the illustrations in this book are not just an elaboration of the verbal text but are an essential aspect of the book's meanings, making this book a true "visual text." The researcher provides in-depth analysis of the illustrations and describes how the story is created through the combination of verbal and visual text.

White, M. (1992). Children's books from other languages: A study of successful translations. *Journal of Youth Services in Libraries*, 5(3), 261–275.

This study identifies the characteristics common to successfully translated children's books. The researcher examines the languages, genres, and subject areas represented, as well as the predominant groups of authors, publishers, illustrators, and translators. Books in German and French, folk tales, and authors such as the Grimm brothers, Astrid Lindgren, and Hans Christian Andersen are the most frequently translated.

Wilson, R. (1987). *Slake's Limbo*: A myth-critical approach. *Children's Literature in Education*, *18*(4), 219–226.

Wilson applies Northrop Frye's notion of literature as displaced myth to an analysis of the adolescent novel *Slake's Limbo* by Felice Holman. This approach may aid students in their own analysis of the text. Especially pertinent to adolescent readers is the consideration of Slake's quest as a journey of adolescent self-discovery.

Other Articles

Austen, H. (1993). Verbal art in children's literature: An application of linguistic theory to the classroom. *English in Australia*, (103), 63–75.

Chaston, J.D. (1992). Flute solos and songs that make you shatter: Simple melodies in *Jacob Have I Loved* and *Come Sing, Jimmy Jo. The Lion and the Unicorn, 16*(2), 215–222.

Doonan, J. (1991). Satoshi Kitamura: Aesthetic dimensions. *Children's Literature, 19*, 107–137.

Dowd, F.A., & Taylor, L.C. (1991). Is there a typical YA fantasy?: A content analysis. *Journal of Youth Services in Libraries, 5*(2), 175–183.

Gannon, S. (1991). The illustrator as interpreter: N.C. Wyeth's illustrations for the adventure novels of Robert Louis Stevenson. *Children's Literature, 19*, 90–106.

Glass, B.J., & Cook, M.K. (1990). Readability of children's periodicals yesterday and today. *Reading Horizons, 30*(3), 224–232.

Goodman, K.S. (1988). Look what they've done to Judy Blume!: The "basalization" of children's literature. *The New Advocate, 1*(1), 29–41.

Kuznets, L. (1985). "High Fantasy" in America: A study of Lloyd Alexander, Ursula LeGuin, and Susan Cooper. *The Lion and the Unicorn, 9*, 19–35.

Mackey, M. (1992). Growing with Laura: Time, space, and the reader in the Little House books. *Children's Literature in Education, 23*(2), 59–74.

Marcus, L.S. (1983–1984). The artist's other eye: The picture books of Mitsumasa Anno. *The Lion and the Unicorn, 7/8*, 34–46.

McGee, T. (1993). ABCs of ABCs: Two Canadian exemplars. *Canadian Children's Literature*, (71), 25–71.

Moss, A. (1985). Mythical narrative: Virginia Hamilton's *The Magical Adventure of Pretty Pearl. The Lion and the Unicorn, 9*, 50–57.

Nodelman, P. (1985). Text as teacher: The beginning of *Charlotte's Web. Children's Literature, 13*, 109–127.

Nodelman, P. (1991). The eye and the E: Identification and first-person narratives in picture books. *Children's Literature, 19*, 1–30.

Nodelman, P. (1993). The illustrators of Munsch. *Canadian Children's Literature*, (71), 5–25.

Paul, L. (1993). The lay of the land: Turbulent flow and Ted Harrison. *Canadian Children's Literature*, (70), 63–71.

Petzold, D. (1992). Wish-fulfillment and subversion: Roald Dahl's Dickensian fantasy *Matilda. Children's Literature in Education, 23*(4), 185–193.

Shaner, M.E. (1992). Instruction and delight: Medieval romances as children's literature. *Poetics Today, 13*(1), 5–15.

Stephens, J. (1990). Intertextuality and *The Wedding Ghost. Children's Literature in Education, 21*(1), 23–36.

Stephens, J. (1993). Metafiction and interpretation: William Mayne's *Salt River Times, Winter Quarters*, and *Drift. Children's Literature, 21*, 101–117.

Susina, J. (1992). The voices of the prairie: The use of music in Laura Ingalls Wilder's *Little House on the Prairie. The Lion and the Unicorn, 16*(2), 158–166.

Tatar, M. (1985). Tests, tasks, and trials in the *Grimm's Fairy Tales. Children's Literature, 13*, 31–48.

Thorpe, D. (1993). "Why don't we see him?": Questioning the frame in illustrated children's stories. *Canadian Children's Literature*, (70), 5–21.

Thuente, M.H. (1985). Beyond historical fiction: Speare's *The Witch of Blackbird Pond*. *English Journal*, 74(6), 50–55.

Woolsey, D.P. (1991). The realm of fairy story: J.R.R. Tolkien and Robin McKinley's *Beauty*. *Children's Literature in Education*, 23(2), 129–135.

Dissertations

Fortuna, M. (1989). *A descriptive evaluative study of children's modern fantasy and children's science fiction using a well-known example of each (Lewis, L'Engle)*. Unpublished doctoral dissertation, Temple University, Philadelphia, PA. (*Dissertation Abstracts International*–A, 49/07, p. 1696)

Fowler, R.B. (1991). *A study of the communication between artist and child through the use of toys in the illustrations of Caldecott Medal books, 1938–1990*. Unpublished doctoral dissertation, University of Alabama, Birmingham. (*Dissertation Abstracts International*–A, 52/06, p. 2016)

Fuller, M.D.M. (1990). *The wordless book: Its relationship to children's literature as perceived by a selected group of principal informants*. Unpublished doctoral dissertation, University of Missouri, Columbia. (*Dissertation Abstracts International*–A, 50/07, p. 1969)

Manhart, M.F. (1991). *Analysis of affixed words: Ten selected trade books*. Unpublished doctoral dissertation, University of Nebraska, Lincoln. (*Dissertation Abstracts International*–A, 52/06, p. 2088)

Sampson, M.B. (1990). *The writing behavior portrayed by selected children's books, basal readers, and classroom teachers.* Unpublished doctoral dissertation, East Texas State University, Commerce. (*Dissertation Abstracts International*–A, 52/02, p. 452)

Swan, A.M. (1991). *An analysis of selected pseudoscientific phenomena in children's literature.* Unpublished doctoral dissertation, University of Akron, OH. (*Dissertation Abstracts International*–A, 51/11, p. 3656)

Historical Research

Historical research focuses on the background of a particular group of books or a specific publication. The history of children's literature can provide insight into current and past trends in the field and understanding about the influence of sociological and historical contexts on the content of the literature. Historical studies follow an issue or phenomenon for a time ranging from 5 to 200 years, often looking closely at social and cultural issues over that period.

Three major types of study are included in this category. The first kind examines the general historical trends in the field of children's literature over time or focuses on the history of a particular group of books, such as African American or French literature. Several studies also consider the history of literature written by and for children. The second type of study looks at the history of a theme, plot element, or character, for example, wolves, happy endings, or Abraham Lincoln. The third type examines the changes in a particular book, such as Pinocchio or Mother Goose tales, over time. Most of these studies also relate the history of children's literature to the sociopolitical issues of different eras.

Most of this research is conducted by university faculty in literary criticism and education, with occasional contributions from library science faculty. The main outlets for publication of these studies are journals that focus on children's literature with a literary criticism or education orientation. A few studies also appear in library science journals. Typically the research requires locating materials in libraries and private collections, where most primary resources are held, and then examining these materials through content analysis.

The history of children's literature is the basis of the field today, and there is always a need for further research to broaden understanding. Comparative studies seem to be one useful way to examine history by comparing attitudes, interests, works, and reading audiences from one period to another. Historical study helps readers see how children's literature reflects a particular society's view of the world and children by comparing the perspectives of authors, illustrators, political figures, and social norms of one time period.

Since historical studies can reveal topics or issues that are not currently being addressed in children's literature, continued research of trends needs to be encouraged. Only a few studies that look at broad trends within the field were found. The field of children's book illustration has undergone tremendous change due to continuing development of new technologies. More research is needed to examine this change as well as the significance of illustration in children's literature and the role of the illustrator across time.

Articles with Annotations

Elleman, B. (1987). Current trends in literature for children. *Library Trends, 35*(3), 413–426.

> Elleman cites sociopolitical upheaval and changes in the field of publishing as the two major influences on children's literature from 1960 to 1985. She examines both positive and negative trends resulting from these influences in fiction, picture books, and nonfiction. She predicts continued growth and quality for the future.

Greenleaf, S. (1992). The beast within. *Children's Literature in Education, 23*(1), 49–57.

> The relationship of children's literature and thinking about the natural world is traced through an examination of books about wolves from the 19th and 20th centuries. The portrayal of wolves in these books is connected to societal values and events and reflects the major stages of

growth in thinking about nature as something to be feared to something to be controlled to something to be respected.

Harris, V. (1990). African American children's literature: The first one hundred years. *Journal of Negro Education, 59*(4), 540–555.

This is a historical review of children's literature written about, for, and by African Americans since the late 1800s. Discussion centers on the significant eras, trends in stereotyping, people who have influenced change, and the socially and culturally conscious literature. Harris also considers trends in more recently published literature and discusses the implications of the lack of these books on the success of all students in school, especially African Americans.

Le Men, S. (1992). Mother Goose illustrated: From Perrault to Doré. *Poetics Today, 13*(1), 17–39.

The author traces the development of the illustration process to the end of the 19th century. Using the frontispiece of Mother Goose in Perrault's original 1697 publication, the study follows trends in illustration to the 1862 publication, in which the frontispiece is done by Doré. Le Men notes such changes in symbolism as a spindle being replaced by a book, indicating a move from an oral to a written tradition.

Little, G. (1992). The care and nurture of aspiring writers: Young contributors to *Our Young Folks* and *St. Nicholas*. *Children's Literature Association Quarterly, 17*(4), 19–23.

This work focuses on the influence editors of the children's magazines *Our Young Folks* and *St. Nicholas* had on their readership of the late 1800s and early 1900s. The discussion centers on the publication of readers' contributions, the role of editors as teachers of good writing, and problems of plagiarism. The study implies that these publications influenced American values and culture.

Mills, C. (1987). Children in search of a family: Orphan novels through the century. *Children's Literature in Education, 18*(4), 227–239.

> Orphan novels have been a mainstay of children's fiction throughout the past century, but there have been significant changes in the image of orphanhood they portray. The effervescent, exuberant orphans of the early 1900s gave way to the passive, polite orphans of the mid-1900s and to the angry, bitter orphans of recent fiction. These changes reflect historical shifts in how society views childhood.

Other Articles

Apseloff, M.F. (1992). Children go west: Fact and fiction. *Children's Literature Association Quarterly, 17*(1), 24–28.

Chaston, J. (1991). American children's fiction of the eighties: Continuity and innovation. *Children's Literature in Education, 22*(4), 223–232.

Donelson, K. (1985). Almost 13 years of book protests...now what? *School Library Journal, 13*(3), 93–98.

Dunn-Lardeau, B. (1992). The shaping of a national identity through history and hagiography in *Notre légende dorée* (Montreal, 1923). *Poetics Today, 13*(1), 63–84.

Ellis, W.G. (1985). Adolescent literature: Changes, cycles, and constancy. *English Journal, 74*(3), 94–98.

Jenkins, C.A. (1993). Young adult novels with gay/lesbian characters and themes 1969–92: A historical reading of content, gender, and narrative distance. *Youth Services in Libraries, 7*(1), 43–55.

Klatt, B. (1992). Abraham Lincoln: Deified martyr, flesh and blood hero, and a man with warts. *Children's Literature in Education, 23*(3), 119–129.

Levstik, L. (1990). From outside in: America's children's literature from 1920–1940. *Theory and Research in Social Education, 18*(4), 327–343.

MacLeod, A.S. (1992). From rational to romantic: The children of children's literature in the nineteenth century. *Poetics Today, 13*(1), 141–153.

Malarte-Feldman, C.L. (1993). A survey of children's literature in France. *Canadian Children's Literature,* (69), 17–30.

Moyles, R.G. (1992). *Adventures in a Sea-Girt Isle*: Creating a Newfoundland-Labrador identity in "early" juvenile fiction. *Canadian Children's Literature,* (66), 7–22.

Osa, O. (1985). The rise of African children's literature. *The Reading Teacher, 38*(8), 750–754.

Paley, N. (1991). Experiments in picture book design: Modern artists who made books for children 1900–1985. *Children's Literature Association Quarterly, 16*(4), 264–269.

Pape, W. (1992). Happy endings in a world of misery: A literary convention between social constraints and utopia in children's and adult literature. *Poetics Today, 13*(1), 179–196.

Rivto, H. (1985). Learning from animals: Natural history for children in the eighteenth and nineteenth centuries. *Children's Literature, 13,* 72–93.

Sadler, D. (1992). Innocent hearts: The child authors of the 1920's. *Children's Literature Association Quarterly, 17*(4), 24–30.

Witucke, V. (1985). Trends in juvenile biography: Five years later. *Top of the News, 42*(1), 45–53.

Wunderlich, R. (1992). The tribulations of *Pinocchio*: How social change can wreck a good story. *Poetics Today, 13*(1), 197–219.

Dissertations

Alqudsi, T.M. (1988). *The history of published Arabic children's literature as reflected in the collections of three publishers in Egypt, 1912–1986*. Unpublished doctoral dissertation, University of Texas, Austin. (*Dissertation Abstracts International*–A, 50/02, p. 285)

Johnson, D.A. (1988). *For the children of the sun: What we say to Afro-American youth through story and image*. Unpublished doctoral dissertation, Yale University, New Haven, CT. (*Dissertation Abstracts International*–A, 50/05, p. 1345)

Kuivasmaki, R. (1990). *A chaste mind with a noble longing for beauty: Finnish-language children's literature, 1851–1899*. Unpublished doctoral dissertation, University of Jyvaskyla, Finland. (*Dissertation Abstracts International*–C, 52/03, p. 307)

Lake, W.M. (1989). *Aspects of Ireland in children's fiction: An historical outline and analysis of children's fiction set in Ireland (1850–1986)*. Unpublished doctoral dissertation, University of Ulster, Coleraine, Northern Ireland. (*Dissertation Abstracts International*–A, 51/11, p. 3754)

Marks, P.A. (1991). *A voice in Ramah: Rhetorical structure and cultural context in 'Uncle Tom's Cabin'*. Unpublished doctoral dissertation, University of Rhode Island, Kingston. (*Dissertation Abstracts International*–A, 52/10, p. 3602)

Miller, C.P. (1990). *Biographies about Abraham Lincoln for children (1865–1969): Portrayals of his parents*. Unpublished doctoral dissertation, University of Illinois, Urbana-

Champaign. (*Dissertation Abstracts International*–A, 51/12, p. 4046)

Sigler, C. (1992). *Wee folk, good folk: Subversive children's literature and British social reform, 1700–1900.* Unpublished doctoral dissertation, Florida State University, Tallahassee. (*Dissertation Abstracts International*–A, 53/03, p. 822)

Stone, J.C. (1990). *The evolution of Civil War novels for children.* Unpublished doctoral dissertation, Ohio State University, Columbus. (*Dissertation Abstracts International*–A, 51/07, p. 2299)

Vandell, K.S. (1991). *The everlasting if: American national identity in children's historical fiction, 1865–1965.* Unpublished doctoral dissertation, University of Maryland, College Park. (*Dissertation Abstracts International*–A, 52/06, p. 2186)

Weir, M.N. (1989). *Inside the ring: Victorian and Edwardian fantasy for children.* Unpublished doctoral dissertation, Simon Fraser University, British Columbia, Vancouver, Canada. (*Dissertation Abstracts International*–A, 53/01, p. 165)

Author and Illustrator Studies

Author and illustrator studies relate a particular book or body of work to the life of its author or illustrator. The researcher gathers material on the life of the author or illustrator and uses the material to analyze that person's work. Sometimes the analysis focuses on the situations and influences from the author's or illustrator's life that affected the writing of one book. Other times the research examines the author's or illustrator's body of work and considers the influence of the person's life on that collection. These studies also address how the literature influences children's thinking in a particular time period.

This research usually involves some type of content analysis, thus allowing researchers to make inferences about themes and topics in the author's or illustrator's work. The content analyses may examine a particular book, illustration, or body of work by an author or compare various authors' styles. In some articles, authors and illustrators examine their own works in relation to current social issues, while other articles investigate how an author's early writing influenced later writing. An additional form of analysis examines the identities and qualifications of authors who are writing a particular genre of literature.

It was difficult to determine which studies to include in this category. Many of the author and illustrator studies refer to a historical era because of its influence on the author's or illustrator's perspective. When the researcher was primarily concerned with the author's or illustrator's life and writing, the study was placed into this category; studies which traced the history of a book with little reference to the author or illustrator were placed under historical research. Studies in which researchers critically analyzed a book by a specific author or illustrator created an additional point of confusion. When the researchers analyzed the writing or illustration of a specific book without reference to the author's or illustrator's life or the sociological or historical context, the study was placed into the text and literary analysis category.

Most of the research in this category was conducted by university faculty who compared or analyzed books, stories, and illustrations of specific authors or illustrators. Recently published studies include more content analyses written by authors and illustrators about their own works. The majority of these articles are found in journals associated with the study of children's literature from a literary criticism perspective rather than an educational perspective.

Although this category includes content analyses of works by authors and illustrators, illustrations and texts of books are usually examined as separate entities. Researchers have rarely examined the picture book as a whole to see how the illustrations and text are interwoven to tell the story. Interesting areas of current research that we hope will continue include studies of authors and illustrators whose work cuts across a range of genres and research by authors and illustrators who analyze and write about their own lives and work.

Although the content analyses in this category include a variety of individual and comparative studies by authors, illustrators, and university researchers, the voices of classroom teachers and students are noticeably absent. It would be productive to expand this research to include the study of authors and illustrators by teacher and student researchers. The articles currently do not include practical applications which might follow from such research. If such applications did appear, it would be easier to incorporate the research findings into classrooms and libraries. Much

of this research is currently ignored by teachers who do not
see its implications for classroom use.

Articles with Annotations

Cleaver, E. (1983–1984). Idea to image: The journey of a
picture book. *The Lion and the Unicorn, 7/8*, 156–170.

> In this study, an illustrator shares her analysis of the
> steps in creating artwork for her books. She is attracted
> to a particular myth or legend because of its verbal or
> visual images. Her themes center on the legends of the
> North American Indians, the folklore of French Canadi-
> ans, and the legends of Hungary.

Fletcher, S. (1993). Why the dracling died. *The New Advocate 6*(4), 243–249.

> The author reviews her own work and talks about her cre-
> ative vision and how that vision relates to her life. She
> has come to the conclusion that even though there is
> choice in writing, she has to write what "feels right." That
> sometimes means letting a character die or suffer in or-
> der for stories to be interesting. She concludes that fic-
> tion draws much of its power from connections to the real
> world and that real-world stories have both happy and
> sad endings.

Storr, C. (1992). *Peter Pan. Children's Literature in Education, 23*(1), 15–26.

> In comparing the book to the play, the author questions
> whether *Peter Pan* has become outdated. The play was
> written from a chapter in James Barrie's book *The Little
> White Bird*, and the story of Peter Pan followed. This re-
> searcher suggests reasons and provides examples as to
> why the play version is superior to the narrative version.
> She also includes examples of how Barrie's life is played
> out in *Peter Pan*.

Susina, J. (1992). "Respiciendo prudens": Lewis Carroll's
juvenilia. *Children's Literature Association Quarterly,
17*(4), 10–14.

This author study examines the influence of Lewis Carroll's early writings on his later well-known works. From the ages of 13 to 23, Carroll was involved in publishing eight "family newspapers," where the beginnings for *Alice's Adventures in Wonderland* can be found. Carroll's interest in the use of puns, parody, and visual images also finds its roots in these early writings.

Other Articles

Blackmore, T. (1993). *Cerebus*: From aardvark to Vanaheim, reaching for creative heaven in David Sim's hellish world. *Canadian Children's Literature*, (71), 57–78.

Bremser, M. (1993). The voice of solitude: The children's verse of Walter de la Mare. *Children's Literature, 21*, 66–91.

Broadway, M.D., & Howland M. (1991). Science books for young people: Who writes them? *School Library Journal, 37*(5), 35–38.

Calish, R. (1986). Mark Twain and the American myth. *English Journal, 75*(6), 60–63.

Cashdan, L. (1989). Powerful levers: Margaret Gatty, Juliana Horatia Ewing, and Mary Louisa Molesworth. *Children's Literature in Education, 20*(4), 215–225.

Culley, J. (1991). Roald Dahl—"It's about children and it's for children"—but is it suitable? *Children's Literature in Education, 22*(1), 59–73.

Edwards, G. (1993). Dayal Kaur Khalsa: The art of remembering. *Canadian Children's Literature*, (70), 48–62.

Hildebrand, A. (1993). Jean de Bruhoff's psychomachia and the doctrine of happiness. *Children's Literature Association Quarterly, 8*(3), 131–136.

Hollindale, P. (1993). Peter Pan: The text and the myth. *Children's Literature in Education, 24*(1), 19–30.

Neumeyer, P. (1985). The creation of E.B. White's *The Trumpet of the Swan*: The manuscripts. *The Horn Book, 61*(1), 17–28.

Plotz, J. (1992). The pet of letters: Marjorie Flemming's juvenilia. *Children's Literature Association Quarterly, 17*(4), 4–9.

Roop, P. (1987). Scott O'Dell: Using history to tell his story. *Children's Literature Association Quarterly, 12*(4), 172–174.

Shealy, D. (1992). Louisa May Alcott's juvenilia: Blueprints of the future. *Children's Literature Association Quarterly, 17*(4), 15–18.

Thompson H. (1993). Transformation and puppetry in the illustrations of Elizabeth Cleaver. *Canadian Children's Literature*, (70), 72–83.

Dissertations

Barlow, D.L. (1989). *The communication of science information to children through trade books: The nature of authorship.* Unpublished doctoral dissertation, University of Maryland, College Park. (*Dissertation Abstracts International*–A, 50/07, p. 1837)

Fondse, C.H. (1988). *The writings of Monica Hughes: Implications for the middle school.* Unpublished doctoral dissertation, Ohio State University, Columbus. (*Dissertation Abstracts International*–A, 48/09, p. 2263)

Heflin, D.D. (1991). *The contribution of Carlota Carvallo's short stories to Peruvian children's literature.* Unpublished doctoral dissertation, Texas Tech University, Lubbock. (*Dissertation Abstracts International*–A, 52/05, p. 1758)

Johnson, D.A. (1991). *Continued success: The early boys' fiction of Edward Stratemeyer and the Stratemeyer syndicate*. Unpublished doctoral dissertation, University of Minnesota, Minneapolis. (*Dissertation Abstracts International*–A, 52/01, p. 197)

Lac, C.M.A. (1988). *Women and children first: A comparative study of Louisa May Alcott and Sophie de Segur*. Unpublished doctoral dissertation, University of Nebraska, Lincoln. (*Dissertation Abstracts International*–A, 50/02, p. 437)

Reading Attitudes and Interests

Knowledge about children's reading interests has proved elusive even though reading interest studies have been conducted with children since the late 1800s. This category of research contains current studies in which researchers are attempting to determine school-age children's interests and attitudes related to reading children's books. Additional research on children's interests can be found in the category of voluntary reading where the focus is on the instructional use of recreational reading to improve students' attitudes and interests.

A range of topics is being researched within this category. One group of studies looks at interests and preferences of particular groups of students for particular types of books. Factors such as hard or soft book covers, the gender of the main character, and the gender of the reader have all been examined. A second group of studies examines the effect of literature on student attitudes about a particular topic or group of people, such as the mentally handicapped or the elderly. Other studies look at students' attitudes toward reading and at programs that lead to more positive attitudes. Research has examined the perceptions and knowledge of students' reading held by children, teachers, and parents. Enthusiasm and interests have also been studied.

Research on attitudes and interests has been published primarily in journals of education and library science. Those conducting this research are usually individuals in a college or university setting in the fields of library science and education. Studies by graduate students have been located as well as some by librarians. A few recent studies have been done by teacher researchers.

This research is international in scope; the studies listed here focused on children from the United States, England, and Australia. Methods used in determining children's attitudes and interests in reading are predominantly surveys, questionnaires, and interviews. Several studies eliminated actual books entirely and used fictitious titles rather than familiar books to determine interest or strategies for selection.

One of the major methodological problems of this research is the difficulty of distinguishing between children's expressed interests and real interests. Many factors, including attitude, setting, parents, teachers, and peers, influence what a child will say about his or her reading interests. When given a choice, a child may state a preference for a particular book, but in reality may not be interested in it.

These studies include a wide variety of contexts and topics, but the lack of research involving the reading of real books is obvious. More study needs to be conducted that expands beyond title selection, lists, and forced-choice expressions of preferences. Many times the procedures of this type of research do not complement or fit into the regular classroom routine, such as when a small sample of students is pulled out of class to participate in part of a study. There is a need for more research by teacher researchers and university researchers who actually spend time observing children, reading their written responses to books, and listening to them discuss the reasons for their attitudes and interests. Much can be discovered by sharing current titles with children and giving them the opportunity for oral and written responses in literature logs and small group discussions. The lack of long-term classroom studies of children's attitudes and interests was immediately evident in this research and has limited educators' knowledge.

Reviews of Research

Huntwork, M. (1990). Why girls flock to Sweet Valley High. *School Library Journal, 36*(3), 137–140.

> The appeal of the Sweet Valley High romance series for teenage girls is examined through a review of research on reading preferences, market research, literary value and appeal of romances, student perceptions of pleasure reading and school reading, and the value of pleasure reading. The author places the review in the context of her concern over her daughter's reading. She concludes that students have the right to their own personal reading but that teachers and parents must encourage students to branch out to other types of reading.

Langerman, D. (1990). Books and boys: Gender preferences and book selection. *School Library Journal, 36*(3), 132–136.

> This article summarizes studies analyzing the relationship of boys' and girls' reading preferences to their reading ability. The study also discusses research analyzing the availability of materials for boys and examines female versus male morality.

Monson, D., & Sebesta, S. (1991). Reading preferences. In J. Flood, J.M. Jensen, D. Lapp, & J.R. Squire (Eds.). *Handbook of research on teaching the English language arts* (pp. 664–673). New York: Macmillan.

> This chapter reviews reading interest research from the earliest study in 1897 to the present. Reading preferences and interests are discussed and compared. The review includes sections on contemporary studies and future research. The authors conclude that research on children's interests has been empirically, not theoretically, driven. To focus research efforts, a worthwhile challenge would be to propose a theoretically based program of work on children's interests.

Articles with Annotations

Bard, T., & Leide, J. (1985). Library books selected by elementary school students in Hawaii as indicated by school library circulation records. *Library and Information Science Research*, *7*(2), 115–143.

> The researchers examined the library circulation records of books selected by students in one elementary school in Hawaii during a 5-year period. The records were analyzed to discover patterns according to sex and grade level, to identify titles, subjects, and types of books circulated frequently, and to determine the circulation of classics and award winning titles, Hawaiiana, and books about Asia or Asian Americans.

Bauer, C., Campbell N., & Troxel, V. (1985). Altering attitudes toward the mentally handicapped through print and nonprint media. *School Library Media Quarterly*, *13*(2), 110–114.

> This study examines the effects of literature on creating positive attitudes toward mentally handicapped children. Students in grades four and seven were divided into groups at each grade level to receive either no instruction or book only, video only, or book and video instruction. A significant positive change was found in the book only group of 4th graders, which led researchers to conclude that reading a high-quality story to 4th graders could be a valuable tool for designing future curricula. The study raises questions about lasting changes in attitudes, generalization to other handicaps, and the possibility of a developmental trend in attitude between 4th and 7th grades.

Bleakley, M., Westerberg, V., & Hopkins K. (1988). The effect of character sex on story interest and comprehension in children. *American Education Research Journal*, *25*(1), 145–155.

> The effect of a main characters' sex on boys' and girls' reading interests and comprehension was studied using 5th grade students. Students were randomly assigned to

read a mystery, adventure, or humorous story. Stories appeared in two versions that were identical except for the sex of the main character. Students completed interest and comprehension measures. The findings indicate that boys prefer stories in which the character is male; girls like stories with female characters, but girls' preferences are not as pronounced. The sex of the main character had no significant effect on comprehension.

Dorotik, M., & Betzold, M. (1992). Expanding literacy for all. *The Reading Teacher, 45*(8), 575–578.

This study describes a program developed to reduce the risk of students becoming future dropouts. It involved matching 3rd grade students in two classrooms with adults in an adult literacy program. Two 4-week units were planned and facilitated in both settings to promote adult literacy and address 3rd grade students' apathetic attitudes toward reading and writing. At intervals, letters were exchanged, and on completion, the groups met. Pre- and posttest inventories as well as written and verbal responses indicated positive changes in attitude toward reading and an additional sense of community as students discovered how people can help one another reach goals.

Fisher, P., & Ayres, G. (1990). A comparison of the reading interests of children in England and the United States. *Reading Improvement, 27*(2), 111–115.

The reading interests of 8- to 11-year-olds in the United States and England were compared by asking children to mark their reading preferences from a list of 44 fictitious book titles and an accompanying book description. American children showed greater interest than English children in the categories of science, poetry, and biographies. The categories of jokes, mystery, crafts, and adventure were popular in both countries. The effect of the reader's sex was found to be the strongest, with girls preferring books concerning jokes, crafts, fairy tales, animals, poetry, and biographies and boys preferring science and sports books.

Gutkecht, B. (1991). Mitigating the effects of negative stereotyping of aging and the elderly in primary grade reading instruction. *Reading Improvement*, 28(1), 44–51.

This study measures attitudes of primary grade students on aging and the elderly as affected by reading instructional material. Information is used from a content analysis of basal reading programs, specifically looking at aging and the elderly. After a pretest, students were exposed to literature in which aging and the elderly are portrayed in a positive light. Results at the end of 6 weeks suggest that children had a more positive attitude toward aging and the elderly through reading this literature.

Isaacs, K. (1992). *Go Ask Alice*: What middle schoolers choose to read. *The New Advocate*, 5(2), 129–143.

The researcher determined through a survey of book choices that middle school students depend more on one another than on adults for reading recommendations. Students chose books by specific authors and by genres as well as by size, number of pages, and cover illustration. They often recognized the literary quality of a book as well. Students' interests were diverse, and their reading choices represented many popular authors of today and the past.

Kutiper, K., & Wilson, P. (1993). Updating poetry preferences: A look at the poetry children really like. *The Reading Teacher*, 47(1), 28–35.

Young children's poetry preferences were examined from a historical perspective through a library circulation study conducted in three elementary schools. The findings support previous preference studies. The researchers found that the same general characteristics of rhythm, rhyme, humor, and easy to understand content appealed to young readers. They also suggest that teachers contribute to the development of children's interest in poetry by supporting and increasing their exposure to it in the early years of schooling.

Swanson, B. (1985). Teacher judgments of first-graders' reading enthusiasm. *Reading Research and Instruction, 25*(1), 41–46.

> This investigation of teachers' judgments shows that their perceptions of reading enthusiasm do not always match those of young students. Teachers' judgments may be based simply on reading achievement. The researchers conclude that reading attitude and achievement may be two separate entities in the early stages of learning to read and, perhaps, should be treated as such.

Other Articles

Allen, A. (1993). The school library media center and the promotion of literature for Hispanic children. *Library Trends, 41*(3), 437–461.

Burgess, S. (1985). Reading but not literate: The Childread Survey. *School Library Journal, 31*(5), 27–30.

Campbell, K., Griswold, D., & Smith, F. (1988). Effects of tradebook covers (hardback or paperback) on individualized reading choices by elementary-age children. *Reading Improvement, 25*(3), 166–178.

Chandler, D., & Aldridge, J. (1992). First graders' attitudes toward reading before and after shared reading experiences with predictable books. *Reading Improvement, 29*(3), 207–208.

Childress, G. (1985). Gender gap in the library: Different choices for boys and girls. *Top of the News, 42*(1), 69–73.

Gerlach, J., & Rinehart, S. (1992). Can you tell a book by its cover? *Reading Horizons, 32*(4), 289–298.

Haynes, C., & Richgels, D. (1992). Fourth graders' literature preferences. *Journal of Educational Research, 85*(4), 208–219.

Hiebert, E., Mervar, K., & Person, D. (1990). Research directions: Children's selections of trade books in libraries and classrooms. *Language Arts, 67*(7), 758–763.

Johnson, C.S., & Gaskins, J. (1992). Reading attitude: Types of materials and specific strategies. *Reading Improvement, 29*(2), 133–139.

Johnson, D., Peer, G., & Baldwin, R. (1984). Protagonist preferences among juvenile and adolescent readers. *Journal of Educational Research, 77*(3), 147–150.

Jose, P., & Brewer, W. (1990). Early grade school children's liking of script and suspense story structures. *Journal of Reading Behavior, 22*(4), 355–373.

Martin, P. (1991). Readers/leaders: Exploring the why. *English Journal, 80*(6), 47–53.

Mellon, C. (1992). "It's the best thing in the world!": Rural children talk about reading. *School Library Journal, 38*(9), 37–40.

Mendoza, A. (1985). Reading to children: Their preferences. *The Reading Teacher, 38*(6), 522–527.

Negin, G. (1989). Parental knowledge of readability and children's reading interests. *Reading Horizons, 29*(2), 123–128.

O'Bryan-Garland, S., & Worley, S. (1986). Reading through laughter and tears: Developing healthy emotions in preadolescents. *Childhood Education, 63*(1), 16–23.

Ollmann, H. (1993). Choosing literature wisely: Students speak out. *Journal of Reading, 36*(8), 648–653.

Pascoe, E., & Gilchrist, M. (1987). Children's responses to literature: Views of children and teachers. *English in Australia, 81*, 55–62.

Russ, K. (1989). Relating reading attitude to reading achievement in an east Los Angeles junior high school. *Reading Improvement, 26*(3), 208–214.

Saracho, O., & Dayton, C. (1989). A factor analysis study of reading attitudes in young children. *Contemporary Educational Psychology, 14*(1), 12–21.

Spangler, K. (1988). Reading choices of native children: An informal analysis. *Reading Horizons, 28*(3), 185–191.

Stewig, J. (1990). Choosing the Caldecott winners: Fifth graders give their reasons. *Journal of Youth Services in Libraries, 3*(2), 128–133.

Stoefen-Fisher, J. (1985). Reading interests of hearing and hearing-impaired children. *American Annals of the Deaf, 130*(4), 291–295.

Tunnell, M., Calder, J., & Justen, J. (1988). A short form reading attitude survey. *Reading Improvement, 25*(2), 146–151.

Wilson, P., & Abrahamson, R. (1988). What children's literature classics do children really enjoy? *The Reading Teacher, 41*(4), 406–411.

Wolfson, B., Manning, G., & Manning, M. (1984). Revisiting what children say their reading interests are. *Reading World, 24*(2), 4–10.

Wray, D. & Lewis, M. (1993). The reading experiences and interests of junior school children. *Children's Literature in Education, 24*(4), 251–263.

Dissertations

Berry, M. (1992). *The personal reading interests of third, fourth, and fifth-grade children in selected Arkansas public schools*. Unpublished doctoral dissertation, University of North Texas, Denton. (*Dissertation Abstracts International*–A, 52/12, p. 4276)

Carter, B.B. (1987). *A content analysis of the most frequently circulated information books in three junior high libraries*. Unpublished doctoral dissertation, University of Houston, TX. (*Dissertation Abstracts International*–A, 49/02, p. 213)

Greenlee, A. (1992). *A comparison of sixth-graders' response to well-reviewed and formula series books*. Unpublished doctoral dissertation, University of Minnesota, Minneapolis. (*Dissertation Abstracts International*–A, 53/02, p. 430)

Haynes, C. (1988). *The explanatory power of content for identifying children's literature preferences*. Unpublished doctoral dissertation, Northern Illinois University, DeKalb. (*Dissertation Abstracts International*–A, 49/12, p. 3617)

Howe, K. (1990). *Children's literature and its effects on cognitive and noncognitive behaviors in elementary social studies*. Unpublished doctoral dissertation, University of Minnesota, Minneapolis. (*Dissertation Abstracts International*–A, 51/12, p. 4044)

Family and Preschool Literacy

This section consolidates the research on the relationship between young children and literature in home and preschool settings, primarily before the children enter kindergarten. While each of these studies could have been classified under topic categories such as read-aloud or reader response research, we chose to set them apart. Age and setting are the unifying factor in these investigations, regardless of the research focus. The significance of young children's early transactions with literature in their literacy development is highlighted, and the distinctiveness of home and preschool settings is recognized. This category also includes a few studies of older students at home.

Education journals publish most of this research, with a small portion also in psychology, children's literature, and learning disability journals. Very few of these studies were in journals on early childhood. Organizations devoted to young children could be more supportive of early childhood educators and instrumental in disseminating related research. We may have failed to identify articles in some early childhood journals as research because the brevity of the articles did not allow us to get a sense of the actual research study. The authors may only have had space to discuss implications or recommendations from their work. These journals may need to make changes in their policies to allow researchers the space they need to discuss their research in more depth.

With very few exceptions, university researchers conducted the research, some occasionally studying their own children and home reading sessions. Teachers and directors of family literacy programs also occasionally research the use of children's literature in their particular settings; however, these studies are much less common. Although some of the family and preschool literacy research continues to use quantitative methodologies, qualitative techniques such as ethnographies, case studies, surveys, and descriptive studies are becoming more prevalent.

All of the research in this category involves reading literature aloud and interaction between adults and children. The two subcategories are based on whether the primary contextual location of this research was in the home or in a preschool setting.

Most of the research in the home focuses on three aspects of book reading sessions in various combinations: the adult reader, the child listener and respondent, and the text itself. Examination of the crucial role of the adult at different times in sessions with children occurs from such vantage points as the adult reader's language, behavior, identity (father or mother), and the book reading strategies used. Other research explores the child as an active constructor of meaning, and examines the influence of factors such as the child's age, conceptual and thought development, questions, responses to literature, and the impact of home reading sessions on school achievement. Aspects of the text under investigation include genre, visual design, format, type of print, discourse structure, and illustrations.

The research on literacy in preschool settings primarily focuses on various aspects of read-alouds, such as adults reading to children, the value of repeated reading, and children's retellings of stories read to them. Through a variety of assessment techniques, studies also examine students' attitudes toward reading, their motivation toward learning to read, and the effects of environment and methodology.

Current research on young children exemplifies the growing recognition of the importance of family and preschool literacy as an area of investigation. However, possibilities for future research do exist. A few studies involve children and families with special needs or from different socioeconomic levels, ethnicities, and cultures. However, more research in these areas would add to our knowledge base, understanding, and appreciation of literature and literacy in home and family environments. In addition, more case studies and longitudinal studies of individual families, children, and classrooms, as well as more research by preschool teachers in their own classrooms, would be enlightening and provide deeper insight into the role of literature in children's literacy development. Current research has focused almost exclusively on demonstrating that if adults read aloud to young children, the children will become successful readers. Further research is needed that focuses on a wider range of issues related to young children and literature.

Research in the Home

Review of Research

Silvern, S. (1985). Parent involvement and reading achievement: A review of research and implications for practice. *Childhood Education, 62*(1), 44–50.

> This review discusses parental practices identified as supporting children's literacy development. The study includes implications for teachers as well as approaches used in successful parent involvement programs.

Books

Fox, C. (1993). *At the very edge of the forest: The influence of literature on storytelling by children*. New York: Cassell.

> This book is a study of the imaginative oral storytelling of five preschool children who had extensive experiences hearing stories read aloud. The stories the children tell

are rich and complex, and the researcher's analyses of their language demonstrate that, at every structural level, early interactions with literature can have enormous linguistic and cognitive consequences. The researcher examines these issues in relation to child language, literacy development, and narrative theory.

Morrow, L.M., Burks, S.P., & Rand, M.K. (Eds.). (1992). *Resources in early literacy development*. Newark, DE: International Reading Association.

This annotated bibliography describes books, book chapters, pamphlets, journals, journal articles, brochures, and videocassettes helpful in enhancing teachers' knowledge about areas related to early literacy. These areas include the home environment, oral language, writing and drawing, learning about print, comprehension, television, assessment, children's literature, play, and computers.

White, D. (1984). *Books before five*. Portsmouth, NH: Heinemann.

This insightful diary, first published in 1954, chronicles the development of literary awareness in a child who was read to from the earliest possible age. Sensitively written by her mother, the diary explores and challenges child development theories.

Articles and Chapters

Altwerger, B., Diehl-Faxon, J., & Dockstader-Anders, K. (1985). Read-aloud events as meaning construction. *Language Arts, 62*(5), 476–484.

Dyads of mothers and their 23-month-olds were observed and taped over 6 months to trace changes in the mother's interaction strategies. Results demonstrate that the mother shifts the responsibility for comprehension to the child by adapting her role from conversational text construction to a closer reading of the print as the child's competence in text construction grows.

Crago, M. (1993). Creating and comprehending the fantastic: A case study of a child from twenty to thirty-five months. *Children's Literature in Education*, *24*(3), 209–221.

> This study examines the difference between the young child's confidence in rejecting fantastical or nonsensical ideas and the same child's puzzled hesitation when confronted with a book that contains fantastical elements. The researcher explores her daughter's recorded remarks in both categories, from 20 months to 2 years 11 months.

Mikkelson, N. (1985). Sendak, *Snow White*, and the child as literary critic. *Language Arts*, *62*(4), 362–373.

> This case study traces a young child's (from about age 3 years 7 months to 5) repeated literary experiences with Maurice Sendak stories and *Snow White*. Results demonstrate how this child builds and synthesizes meaning, tests her ideas, and compares and revises them as all discerning critics do.

Pellegrini, A.D., Perlmutter, J.C., Galda, L., & Brody, G.H. (1990). Joint reading between black Head Start children and their mothers. *Child Development*, *61*(2), 443–453.

> The behaviors of black children and their mothers in the Head Start program are studied in a series of experimental joint reading contexts in their homes. Specifically, the study examines the effect of text genre and format on mothers' teaching strategies and their effectiveness in eliciting children's participation in the joint reading tasks.

Smolkin, L.B., Yaden, D.B., Brown, L., & Hofius, B. (1992). The effects of genre, visual design choices, and discourse structure on preschoolers' responses to picture books during parent-child read-alouds. In C.K. Kinzer & D.J. Leu (Eds.), *Literacy research, theory, and practice: Views from many perspectives* (41st yearbook of the National Reading Conference, pp. 291–301). Chicago, IL: National Reading Conference.

In order to explore parent-child discourse structures during read-alouds and preschoolers' responses to visual design and genre, the researchers audiotaped three boys and three girls, ages 3 years 6 months to 4 years 8 months, from upper–middle-class white families over three consecutive 10-day periods. Parents followed regular storybook reading habits with a different set of three books in each 10-day segment. Results indicate that visual design and genre influence children's responses to print and that particular genres affect parent-child discourse.

Snow, C.E., & Nino, A. (1986). The contracts of literacy: What children learn from learning to read books. In W.H. Teale & E. Sulzby (Eds.), *Emergent literacy: Writing and reading* (pp. 116–138). Norwood, NJ: Ablex.

This chapter combines the independent investigations of two researchers to examine the contribution of parent-child book reading interactions to the child's literacy development. Also discussed are the seven basic "contracts of literacy" children learn in these book reading sessions.

Sorsby, A.J., & Martlew, M. (1991). Representational demands in mothers' talk to preschool children in two contexts: Picture book reading and a modelling task. *Journal of Child Language, 18,* 373–395.

A group of 24 mother and child (mean age 4 years 2 months) dyads was videotaped during a play dough modeling task and while reading two books to examine the extent to which the children engaged in abstract thought in these discourse situations. Utterances were transcribed and analyzed. Results indicate that more of the conversation was at a higher level of abstraction during the reading task.

Taylor, D. (1986). Creating family story: "Matthew! We're going to have a ride!". In W.H. Teale & E. Sulzby (Eds.), *Emergent literacy: Writing and reading* (pp. 139–155). Norwood, NJ: Ablex.

The researcher studied audiotapes, constructed with the assistance of the parent, to understand what happens during family story reading. The narrative account of a mother and her three children reveals how the family uses conversation to create the story and learn about themselves and the social world.

Wepner, S.B., & Caccavale, P.P. (1991). Project CAPER (Children And Parents Enjoy Reading): A case study. *Reading Horizons, 31*(3), 228–237.

Project CAPER is a school-home partnership designed to encourage parents to model reading behavior with their children in an effort to make reading part of the children's everyday habits. During the 7 months of the project, 200 volunteer parent-child teams from a New Jersey school district read together daily and individually recorded the title of the material and the amount of time spent reading. Results demonstrate an improvement in students' attitudes toward reading and themselves as readers.

Wolf, S.A. (1991). Following the trail of story. *Language Arts, 68*(5), 388–395.

This case study follows one young child's responses to *Hansel and Gretel* over 4 years through different editions of the tale and multiple changes in the child's interpretation. The researcher uses the data to show how her daughter's responses changed across time and settings and to argue that being literate means being thoughtful, not developing interpretations that match those of the "experts."

Other Articles

Andrews, J.F., & Taylor, N.E. (1987). From sign to print: A case study of picture book "reading" between mother and child. *Sign Language Studies, 56*, 261–274.

Beals, D., & DeTemple, J. (1993). Home contributions to early language and literacy development. In D.J. Leu & C.K. Kinzer (Eds.), *Examining central issues in literacy research, theory, and practice* (42nd yearbook of the National Reading Conference, pp. 207–215). Chicago, IL: National Reading Conference.

Bryant, P.E., Bradley, L., Maclean, M., & Crossland, J. (1989). Nursery rhymes, phonological skills and reading. *Journal of Child Language, 16*(2), 407–428.

Crago, H. (1985). The roots of response. *Children's Literature Association Quarterly, 10*(3), 100–104.

Danielson, K.E. (1992). Learning about early writing from response to literature. *Language Arts, 69*(4), 274–280.

Eldridge-Hunter, D. (1992). Intergenerational literacy: Impact on the development of the storybook reading behaviors of Hispanic mothers. In C.K. Kinzer & D.J. Leu (Eds.), *Literacy research, theory, and practice: Views from many perspectives* (41st yearbook of the National Reading Conference, pp. 101–110). Chicago, IL: National Reading Conference.

Fagan, W., & Hayden, H. (1986). Reading books with young children: Opportunities for concept development. *Australian Journal of Reading, 9*(1), 11–19.

Fagan, W., & Hayden, H. (1988). Parent-child interaction in favorite and unfamiliar stories. *Reading Research and Instruction, 27*(2), 47–55.

Feitelson, D., & Goldstein, Z. (1986). Patterns of book ownership and reading to young children in Israeli school-oriented and nonschool-oriented families. *The Reading Teacher, 39*(9), 924–930.

Goodman, G. (1987). James' grandfathers. *Language Arts, 64*(1), 40–53.

Handel, R.D. (1992). The partnership for family reading: Benefits for families and schools. *The Reading Teacher, 46*(2), 116–126.

Hartle-Schutte, D. (1993). Literacy development in Navajo homes: Does it lead to success in school? *Language Arts, 70*(8), 642–654.

Haussler, M.M., & Jeanne, L.M. (1987). Young Hopi writers and readers. *National Association for Bilingual Education Journal, 11*(2), 83–93.

Lamme, L.L., & Packer, A.B. (1986). Bookreading behavior of infants. *The Reading Teacher, 39*(6), 504–509.

Lazzari, A.M., Bender, W.N., & Kello, M.N. (1987). Parents' and children's behavior during preschool reading sessions as predictors of language and reading skills. *Reading Improvement, 24*(2), 89–95.

Lowe, V. (1991). "Stop! You didn't read who wrote it!": The concept of author. *Children's Literature in Education, 22*(2), 79–88.

Manning, M., Manning, G., & Cody, C.B. (1988). Reading aloud to young children: Perspectives of parents. *Reading Research and Instruction, 27*(2), 56–61.

Paratore, J. (1993). An intergenerational approach to literacy: Effects on the literacy learning of adults and on the practice of family literacy. In D.J. Leu & C.K. Kinzer (Eds.), *Examining central issues in literacy research, theory, and practice* (42nd yearbook of the National Reading Conference, pp. 83–92). Chicago, IL: National Reading Conference.

Pellegrini, A.D., Brody, G.H., & Sigel, I.E. (1985). Parents' book-reading habits with their children. *Journal of Educational Psychology, 77*(3), 332–340.

Penfold, K., & Bacharach, V.R. (1988). Reading to very young children: The impact of illustrations in children's books. *International Journal of Early Childhood, 20*(1), 35–44.

Phillips, G., & McNaughton, S. (1990). The practice of storybook reading to preschool children in mainstream New Zealand families. *Reading Research Quarterly, 25*(3), 196–212.

Porterfield-Stewart, J. (1993). Book reading interactions: What parents and children say. *Reading Horizons, 33*(1), 13–31.

Resnick, M.B., Roth, J., Aaron, P.M., Scott, J., Wolking, W.D., Larsen, J.J., & Packer, A.B. (1987). Mothers reading to infants: A new observational tool. *The Reading Teacher, 40*(9), 888–894.

Roser, N., & Martinez, M. (1985). Roles adults play in preschoolers' response to literature. *Language Arts, 62*(5), 485–490.

Scarborough, H.S., Dobrich, W., & Hager, M. (1991). Preschool literacy experience and later reading achievement. *Journal of Learning Disabilities, 24*(8), 508–511.

Smolkin, L.B., Conlon, A., & Yaden, D.B. (1988). Print salient illustrations in children's picture books: The emergence of written language awareness. In J. Readence & R.S. Baldwin (Eds.), *Dialogues in literacy research* (37th yearbook of the National Reading Conference, pp. 59–68). Chicago, IL: National Reading Conference.

Smolkin, L.B., & Yaden, D.B. (1992). *O is for mouse*: First encounters with the alphabet book. *Language Arts, 69*(6), 432–441.

Voss, M. (1993). "I just watched": Family influences on one child's learning. *Language Arts, 70*(8), 632–641.

Warren, J.S., Prater, N.J., & Griswold, D.L. (1990). Parental practices of reading aloud to preschool children. *Reading Improvement, 27*(1), 41–45.

Wolf, S.A., & Heath, S.B. (1993). The net of a story. *The Horn Book Magazine, 69*(6), 705–713.

Yaden, D.B. (1988). Understanding stories through repeated read-alouds: How many does it take? *The Reading Teacher, 41*(6), 556–560.

Yaden, D.B., Smolkin, L.B., & Conlon, A. (1989). Preschoolers' questions about pictures, print conventions, and story text during reading aloud at home. *Reading Research Quarterly, 24*(2), 188–214.

Yaden, D.B., Smolkin, L.B., & MacGillivray, L. (1993). A psychogenetic perspective on children's understanding about letter associations during alphabet book readings. *Journal of Reading Behavior, 25*(1), 43–68.

Dissertation

Buchanan-Berrigan, D.L. (1989). *Using children's books with adults: Negotiating literacy.* Unpublished doctoral dissertation, Ohio State University, Columbus. (*Dissertation Abstracts International*–A, 50/12, p. 3874)

Research in Preschool Settings

Articles with Annotations

Cochran-Smith, M. (1985). Looking like readers, talking like readers. *Theory into Practice, 24*(1), 22–31.

> This researcher collected ethnographic data for 18 months in a study of the literary and literacy socialization of 3- to 5-year-old children. The analysis examines group story reading and the relationship between the

nonverbal "looking like readers" and verbal "talking like readers" behaviors of young children.

Martinez, M., & Roser, N. (1985). Read it again: The value of repeated readings during storytime. *The Reading Teacher, 38*(8), 782–786.

> Adults read six different stories three times each to children in a home and a preschool setting. The interaction between the adult and child was classified in order to analyze the changes that occurred in the dialogue during repeated readings. This study concludes that when students have more opportunities to hear a story, they begin to focus on different aspects of the story and their range of responses increases.

Mason, J., Kerr, B., & Sinha, S. (1991). Shared book reading in an early start program for at-risk children. In J. Zutell & S.M. McCormick (Eds.), *Learner factors/teacher factors: Issues in literacy research and instruction* (41st yearbook of the National Reading Conference, pp. 189–197). Chicago, IL: National Reading Conference.

> Preschool teachers used "little books" for an informal shared reading activity with one group of children and not another. The little books were used in the classroom, and a copy of the book was sent home with the child at the end of each week. At the end of the year, students using the little books scored significantly higher than the control group on letter knowledge and interest in literacy.

Morrow, L.M. (1987). The effects of one-to-one story readings on children's questions and responses. In J. Readence & R. Baldwin (Eds.), *Research in literacy: Merging perspectives* (36th yearbook of the National Reading Conference, pp. 75–83). Rochester, NY: National Reading Conference.

> This experimental study compares the interactive behaviors of two groups of lower socioeconomic preschoolers. The children in the experimental group were read to individually once a week. The children in the control

group received individual attention but did not participate in read-aloud events. The results show a statistically significant difference between the groups in the areas of interpretive responses and story structure.

Sulzby, E. (1985). Children's emergent reading of favorite storybooks: A developmental study. *Reading Research Quarterly, 20*(4), 458–481.

Kindergarten and preschool children were asked to choose a favorite book and then "read" it to an interviewer. The readings were categorized according to Sulzby's "Categories of Storybook Reading." Developmental trends are noted across the different age levels, with kindergarten children showing significant improvement in their emergent reading across the year.

Other Articles and Chapters

Clyde, J.A., Condon, M.W.F., Daniel, K., & Sommer, M.K. (1993). Learning through whole language: Exploring book selection and use with preschoolers. In L. Patterson, C.M. Santa, K.G. Short, & K. Smith (Eds.), *Teachers are researchers: Reflection and action* (pp. 42–50). Newark, DE: International Reading Association.

Elster, C.A., & Walker, C.A. (1992). Flexible scaffolds: Shared reading and rereading of story books in Head Start classrooms. In C.K. Kinzer & D.J. Leu (Eds.), *Literacy research, theory, and practice: Views from many perspectives* (41st yearbook of the National Reading Conference, pp. 445–452). Chicago, IL: National Reading Conference.

Fox, C. (1985). The book that talks. *Language Arts, 62*(4), 374–384.

Freeman, E.B., & Wasserman, V. (1986). A will before there's a way: Preschoolers and books. *Reading Horizons, 27*(2), 112–122.

Galda, L., Pellegrini, A.D., & Cox, S. (1989). A short-term longitudinal study of preschoolers' emergent literacy. *Research in the Teaching of English, 23*(3), 292–309.

Mallan, K. (1993). 'Once there was a story about three turtles': Oral narrative styles of pre-school children. *The Australian Journal of Language and Literacy, 16*(3), 249–260.

Morrow, L.M. (1988). Young children's responses to one-to-one story reading in school settings. *Reading Research Quarterly, 23*(1), 89–107.

Morrow, L.M. (1989). The effect of small group story reading on children's questions and comments. In S. McCormick & J. Zutell (Eds.), *Cognitive and social perspectives for literacy research and instruction* (38th yearbook of the National Reading Conference, pp. 77–86). Chicago, IL: National Reading Conference.

Roser, N.L. (1987). Research currents: Relinking literature and literacy. *Language Arts, 64*(1), 90–97.

Rottenberg, C.J., & Searfoss, L.W. (1992). Becoming literate in a preschool class: Literacy development of hearing-impaired children. *Journal of Reading Behavior, 24*(4), 463–479.

Saracho, O.N. (1986). The development of the preschool reading attitudes scale. *Child Study Journal, 16*(2), 113–124.

Saracho, O.N., & Dayton, C.M. (1991). Age-related changes in reading attitudes of young children: A cross-cultural study. *Journal of Research in Reading, 14*(1), 33–45.

Senechal, M., & Cornell, E. (1993). Vocabulary acquisition through shared reading experiences. *Reading Research Quarterly, 28*(4), 361–374.

Dissertations

James, A.H. (1987). *Factors influencing teachers' selection of books for preschool children: The purposes and uses of books in the classroom.* Unpublished doctoral dissertation, University of Louisville, KY. (*Dissertation Abstracts International*–A, 49/04, p. 723)

Shea, M.E. (1992). *Children's concepts of print prior to formal instruction.* Unpublished doctoral dissertation, State University of New York, Buffalo. (*Dissertation Abstracts International*–A, 53/05, p. 1391)

Literature-Based Curriculum

Many teachers are moving toward greater use of literature in their classrooms, and curriculum developers are putting together programs based around literature. The research included in this section examines these classrooms and curricula to study their use of children's literature as the primary reading material in reading and language arts or the content areas. These studies do not examine a specific instructional activity or strategy but look more broadly at the curriculum or program and the actions and beliefs of teachers related to literature.

Most of these studies are published in journals of education, reading education, and English education. The primary investigators are university researchers, although in recent years there has been an increase in the number of classroom teacher and student researchers.

A large number of studies focus on the primary grades. We were able to locate some studies of the upper elementary grades, but we found very few that describe literature use in the middle school. The usual context for these studies is within actual classrooms and their curriculum; however, researchers sometimes take students out of the classroom environment to perform studies that do not relate to the curriculum.

Research designs include experimental studies using pre- and posttests, questionnaires, and surveys to compare two types of reading programs. Much of the current research, however, consists of qualitative research designs, such as case studies and descriptions of particular classrooms and literature programs. The primary data sources include ethnographic techniques, such as audio and video transcripts of interviews and discussions, field notes of classroom observations, journal entries, and written arti-facts.

The subcategories of this section include descriptions of literature-based classrooms, comparisons of approaches to teaching reading, the use of literature across the curriculum, and teachers' beliefs and practices. The results of these studies substantiate the value of using literature for classroom instruction in a variety of contexts and across age levels.

Descriptions of Literature-Based Classrooms contains studies depicting classrooms using literature rather than textbooks as the base for instruction. Most of these studies describe various components found in literature-based classrooms and programs rather than examine a broader focus on the different roles literature can play across the curriculum. Some examine the theory and practice behind literature-based reading instruction, links between children and books in creating communities of learners, and the implementation and expanded use of literature-based reading instruction in schools.

Comparisons of Approaches compares literature-based instruction with one or more other methods. These are typically experimental studies in which student performance in skills-oriented or basal reader programs are compared in some way to the performance of students in literature-based classrooms. The definitions of what is considered a literature-based classroom vary considerably in this research. Sometimes, the term refers to a basal reader approach that uses a literature anthology or actual books in combination with workbooks and skills instruction. Other times, it refers to more holistic approaches in which students choose what to read as well as engage in discussions with peers to collaboratively negotiate meaning. These studies focus on literature only as part of the reading program and do not look at its use throughout the curriculum. Some researchers have criticized the use of experimental designs and dependent measures in this research because they feel it is at theoretical variance with holistic literature-based programs and does not measure the actual impact of these programs on children's learning.

Literature Across the Curriculum includes studies that describe the use of children's literature rather than textbooks for content area instruction. Several studies cite the use of literature to teach social studies, and one focuses on its use to teach mathematical concepts. These studies take students' interests into account, and most use some type of inquiry model to support student learning and curriculum.

The studies found in Teachers' Beliefs and Practices document teachers' beliefs about literature and their transition from basals to a literature-based approach to reading. The research also examines the advantages and disadvantages of implementing literature-based instruction. Most of these studies use ethnographic research methodologies and overwhelmingly show the need for a variety of resources—including administrative support, available materials, and theoretical understandings of literature and its use in the classroom—for teachers using literature-based instruction.

There is an abundance of research dealing with curricular issues of literature. Most of this research is quite informative and would greatly benefit those who are interested in literature and its use. However, future research must address some existing gaps, such as studies depicting literature use in settings other than elementary classrooms and use with a greater variety of populations and a wider array of issues, including exceptional populations, middle school students, and multicultural issues. In addition, a number of these studies take place over a very short duration, in some cases, only a matter of days. Observing participants over a longer period would provide a more accurate picture of the beneficial effects of literature in classroom instruction.

Another major issue across these studies is the assumption that the primary role of literature in the classroom is a "better way to teach reading." While we do not disagree with this role of literature, we feel it limits the potentials of literature within the classroom and the connections children can make from their reading. We believe literature can play at least four roles within the curriculum: (1) literature as a way to learn language, especially reading and writing, (2) literature as a way to learn about other content areas and topics such as social studies and science, (3) literature as a way to critique the world through exploring social, political, and cultural issues, and (4) literature as its own way of knowing (Short, 1994). The research on literature-based classrooms has almost exclusively focused on the first role. We did find a few studies that looked at literature as a way to learn about other content and to critique the world, but did not locate any studies that included literature as its own way of knowing or looked at all four roles of literature in the curricuium.

Reference

Short, K.G. (1994). Moving toward literature based curriculum. In A. Flurkey & R. Meyer (Eds.), *Under the Whole Language Umbrella*. Urbana, IL: National Council of Teachers of English.

Reviews of Research

Galda, L., & Cullinan, B. (1991). Literature for literacy: What research says about the benefits of using trade books in the classroom. In J. Flood, J. Jensen, D. Lapp, & J. Squire, *Handbook of Research on Teaching the English Language Arts*, (pp. 529–535). New York: Macmillan.

> This review summarizes research studies that explore the reasons for using literature as an integral component of instruction. The first section examines research on the preschool years in the home and preschool settings. The

second section reviews research on the school years, including studies on interest, language development, reading achievement, composing, and social context. The third section summarizes research on literature-rich classrooms and teacher behaviors.

Tunnell, M., & Jacobs, J. (1989). Using "real" books: Research findings on literature based reading instruction. *The Reading Teacher, 42*(7), 470–477.

This review includes studies that compare literature-based reading programs to basal reader programs as well as studies of literature programs with limited English speakers, students experiencing difficulty with reading, and students labeled "good" readers. Common elements of literature-based reading programs are discussed along with research studies on these elements.

Descriptions of Literature-Based Classrooms

Reviews of Research

Giddings, L.R. (1992). Literature-based reading instruction: An analysis. *Reading Research and Instruction, 31*(2), 18–30.

Giddings reviews articles focusing on literature-based instruction. The term "literature-based reading instruction" is defined, and a theoretical base for such instruction is developed from the research review.

Lehman, B.A., & Crook, P.R. (1988). Effective schools research and excellence in reading: A rationale for children's literature in the curriculum. *Childhood Education, 64*(4), 235–242.

A review of research on effective schools and reading is used to support the belief that children's literature should be incorporated into reading instruction. The authors state that teachers need to use more than basals to teach reading, and they offer ideas on how to use children's literature to do so.

McGee, L.M. (1992). Focus on research: Exploring the literature-based reading revolution. *Language Arts, 69*(7), 529–537.

This article reviews research on literature-based classrooms, primarily studies which involve reader response. McGee also focuses on the necessary process of change for a teacher who moves from a traditional model of teaching to a literature-based model.

Wells, G. (1990). Creating the conditions to encourage literate thinking. *Educational Leadership, 47*(6), 13–17.

Some of the key insights from recent research on literacy are summarized to explore what it means to be literate, how literacy is acquired, and the educational conditions that create classroom communities of literate thinkers.

Book

Applebee, A.N. (1993). *Literature in the secondary school: Studies of curriculum and instruction in the United States.* Urbana, IL: National Council of Teachers of English.

This book reports on four major studies of current practices in the teaching of literature in middle and secondary schools. Findings conclude that literary curriculum is neither as good as hoped or as poor as critics claim. Applebee calls for a thorough reexamination of literature curriculum to provide teachers with a more unified framework that will better inform their practice.

Articles with Annotations

Hade, D.D. (1991). Being literary in a literature-based classroom. *Children's Literature in Education, 22*(1), 1–17.

Hade states that authenticity is the key to using real texts for teaching reading. He describes effective literary classrooms, and he lists the components needed to help children to become lifelong readers. The author has arrived at this list through reading, research, and observation. He cites entries from his field notes to support his conclusions.

Hall, D.P., & Cunningham, P.M. (1992). Reading without ability grouping: Issues in first-grade reading instruction. In C.K. Kinzer & D.J. Leu (Eds.). *Literacy research, theory, and practice: Views from many perspectives* (41st yearbook of the National Reading Conference, pp. 235–241). Chicago, IL: National Reading Conference.

Six 1st grade teachers from two schools implemented a non-ability group reading program. The program they designed has four components: (1) classwide use of the same basal and workbook pages with a partner, (2) a self-selected reading block for reading books of the students' choice, (3) a writing block beginning with a 5–10 minute minilesson in which the teacher models the writing process, and (4) Working with Words, a spelling program for high frequency words. All students showed growth at the end of the year, with no students being labeled as nonreaders.

Nix, K. (1987). On producing brand-new book lovers. *Children's Literature Association Quarterly, 12*(3), 131–134.

The researcher initiated a literature program in a private school, beginning with 3rd grade and continuing with successive grades each year. She worked in classrooms discussing books and reading aloud to students, as well as in the library helping students select books. Homework required the children to read for 30 minutes each night during 5 nights a week in a variety of genres. The program most consistently reached students who were not reading due to lack of exposure and experience. Similar results occurred when the researcher instituted this literature program in an inner-city school.

Oldfather, P. (1993). What students say about motivating experiences in a whole language classroom. *The Reading Teacher, 46*(8), 672–681.

This study takes place in a 5th and 6th grade combination classroom and focuses on students' descriptions of their reasons for being motivated to learn. Much of their motivation stems from having the freedom to choose what they want to learn. Students are encouraged to link their classroom experiences to their own lives and to be self-expressive through their writing, discussions of their reading, group projects, and fine arts. Comments from students show how they feel empowered to learn through these activities.

Other Articles

Bartley, N. (1993). Literature-based integrated language instruction and the language-deficient student. *Reading Research and Instruction, 32*(2), 31–37.

Cullinan, B.E. (1989). Latching on to literature: Reading initiative takes hold. *School Library Journal, 35*(8), 27–31.

Cunningham, P.M. (1991). Research directions: Multimethod, multilevel literacy instruction in first grade. *Language Arts, 68*(7), 578–584.

Hughes, S.M. (1993). The impact of whole language on four elementary school libraries. *Language Arts, 70*(5), 393–399.

Nystrand, M., & Gamoran, A. (1991). Instructional discourse, student engagement, and literature achievement. *Research in the Teaching of English, 25*(3), 261–291.

Robb, L. (1993). A cause for celebration: Reading and writing with at-risk students. *The New Advocate, 6*(1), 25–40.

Skolnick, D.F. (1992). Reading relationships. *The New Advocate, 5*(2), 117–127.

Smith, J.L., & Johnson, H.A. (1993). Control in the classroom: Listening to adolescent voices. *Language Arts, 70*(1), 18–30.

Walmsley, S.A. (1992). Reflections on the state of elementary literature instruction. *Language Arts, 69*(7), 508–514.

Dissertations

Canavan, D. (1992). *The nature of reading instruction in a literature-based reading program.* Unpublished doctoral dissertation, University of North Texas, Denton. (*Dissertation Abstracts International–A*, 53/08, p. 2752)

Jenkins, L.S. (1991). *The children's literature curriculum of an elementary school: A microethnography.* Unpublished doctoral dissertation, Florida State University, Tallahassee. (*Dissertation Abstracts International–A*, 52/10, p. 3525)

Nussbaum, N.R. (1990). *Exploring literacy: Apprenticeship in a first grade classroom of an inner city school.* Unpublished doctoral dissertation, Ohio State University, Columbus. (*Dissertation Abstracts International–A*, 51/11, p. 3687)

Reimer, K.M. (1991). *Literature as the core of the reading curriculum: Multiple perspectives.* Unpublished doctoral dissertation, University of Illinois, Urbana-Champaign. (*Dissertation Abstracts International–A*, 52/07, p. 2446)

Strong, E.L. (1988). *Nurturing early literacy: A literature based program for at-risk first graders.* Unpublished doctoral dissertation, Ohio State University, Columbus. (*Dissertation Abstracts International–A*, 49/09, p. 2528)

Troyer, C.R. (1992). *Language in first-grade: A study of reading, writing, and talking in school.* Unpublished doctoral dissertation, Northern Illinois University, DeKalb. (*Dissertation Abstracts International–A*, 53/06, p. 1855)

Zarrillo, J.J. (1988). *Literature-centered reading programs in elementary classrooms.* Unpublished doctoral dissertation, The Claremont Graduate School, CA. (*Dissertation Abstracts International*–A, 49/06, p. 1366)

Comparison of Approaches

Articles with Annotations

Bader, L.A., Veatch, J., & Eldredge, J.L. (1987). Trade books or basal readers? *Reading Improvement, 24*(1), 62–67.

> The researchers conducted five experiments to compare literature-based reading programs with basal reading programs. They also compared homogeneous grouping and heterogeneous grouping as well as analytic phonics instruction and analytical and synthetic phonics instruction. Results indicate that students' achievement and interests were strongly and positively affected by the use of children's literature, analytical and synthetic phonics instruction, and heterogeneous grouping.

Chandler, J., & Baghban, M. (1986). Predictable books guarantee success. *Reading Horizons, 26*(3), 167–173.

> This study compares the use of basals with the use of predictable books for reading instruction in 1st, 2nd, and 3rd grade classrooms. The control group followed the sequential skills recommended by the Ginn Reading Series, and the experimental group used a modified version of Stauffer's Directed Reading–Thinking Approach. Results show that students in the experimental group improved significantly over those in the control group.

Elley, W.B. (1991). Acquiring literacy in a second language: The effect of book-based programs. *Language Learning, 41*(3), 375–411.

> The article briefly reviews nine studies conducted by the researcher in the South Pacific and Southeast Asia. Comparisons were made between programs based on structured, systematic second-language instruction and programs that exposed children to large amounts of high interest literature. The literature immersion programs al-

lowed children to learn language incidentally and to develop positive attitudes toward books. Additional research studies on literature and second-language learners are briefly summarized.

Fischer, C.W., & Hiebert, E.H. (1990). Characteristics of tasks in two approaches to literacy instruction. *The Elementary School Journal, 91*(1), 3–18.

Fischer and Hiebert describe the differences between two classrooms with a skills-oriented approach to literacy and two classrooms with a literature-based approach to literacy. Data collection over 5 days of instruction includes videotapes, field notes, teacher interviews, and samples of student artifacts. Results indicate that opportunities for engaging with literature varied over time and amount between the two approaches. Students in the literature-based classrooms shared in the decision making process and had more opportunities to engage with literacy experiences.

Hiebert, E.H., Mervar, K.B., & Person, D. (1990). Research directions: Children's selection of trade books in libraries and classrooms. *Language Arts, 67*(7), 758–763.

Hiebert, Mervar, and Person describe the strategies of second graders from literature-based classrooms and text-based classrooms for self-selecting books. Students were observed and interviewed during selection time in both their school libraries and classrooms. Results indicate that the students from the literature-based classrooms were able to articulate in greater depth their reason for selection. The researchers further describe the kinds of guidance received from the classroom teachers and from librarians and suggest ways to connect these two contexts. They conclude by recommending that connections between the classroom and library also need to include the home.

Other Articles

Dahl, K.L., & Freppon, P.A. (1987). Literacy learning in whole-language classrooms: An analysis of low socioeconomic urban children learning to read and write in kindergarten. In J. Readence & R.S. Baldwin (Eds.), *Research in literacy: Merging perspectives* (36th yearbook of the National Reading Conference, pp. 1–332). Rochester, NY: National Reading Conference.

DeWalt, M., Riyne-Winkler, M.C., & Rubel, S. (1993). Effects of instructional method on reading. *Reading Improvement, 30*(2), 93–98.

Eldredge, J.L., & Butterfield, D. (1986). Alternatives to traditional reading instruction. *The Reading Teacher, 40*(1), 32–37.

Freppon, P.A. (1991). Children's concepts of the nature and purpose of reading in different instructional settings. *Journal of Reading Behavior, 23*(2), 139–163.

Hiebert, E.H., Colt, J.M., Catto, S.L., & Gury, E.C. (1992). Reading and writing of first-grade students in a restructured Chapter 1 program. *American Educational Research Journal, 29*(3), 545–572.

Klesius, J.P., Griffith, P.L., & Zielonka, P. (1991). A whole language and traditional instruction comparison: Overall effectiveness and development of the alphabetic principle. *Reading Research and Instruction, 30*(2), 47–61.

Milligan, J.L., & Berg, H. (1992). The effect of whole language on the comprehending ability of first grade children. *Reading Improvement, 29*(3), 146–154.

Morrow, L.M. (1992). The impact of a literature-based program on literacy achievement, use of literature, and attitudes of children from minority backgrounds. *Reading Research Quarterly, 27*(3), 251–275.

Nystrand, M. (1991). Instructional discourse, student engagement, and literature achievement. *Research in the Teaching of English, 25*(3), 261–290.

Phillips, L.M., Norris, S.P., Mason, M.M., & Kerr, B.M. (1991). Effect of early literacy intervention on kindergarten achievement. In J. Zutell, & S. McCormick (Eds.), *Learner factors/teacher factors: Issues in literacy research and instruction* (40th yearbook of the National Reading Conference, pp. 199–207). Chicago, IL: National Reading Conference.

Rasinski, T.V., & DeFord, D.E. (1988). First graders' conception of literacy: A matter of schooling. *Theory Into Practice, 27*(1), 53–61.

Stahl, S.A., & Miller, P.D. (1989). Whole language and language experience approaches for beginning reading: A quantitative research synthesis. *Review of Educational Research, 59*(1), 87–116.

Dissertations

Bryan, M.C. (1990). *Exploring the relationship of whole language and isolated skill instruction with reading and writing skills of intermediate remedial readers.* Unpublished doctoral dissertation, University of North Dakota, Grand Forks. (*Dissertation Abstracts International*–A, 52/02, p. 485)

Curry, L.J. (1991). *A literature-based language curriculum in public Montessori.* Unpublished doctoral dissertation, Texas A&M University, College Station. (*Dissertation Abstracts International*–A, 52/02, p. 408)

Literature Across the Curriculum

Articles with Annotations

Kliman, M., & Kleiman, G.M. (1992). Life among the giants: Writing, mathematics, and exploring Gulliver's world. *Language Arts, 69*(2), 128–136.

> This research reports the field testing of a curriculum unit based on *Gulliver's Travels* focusing on the integration of literature, writing, and mathematics in 10 upper elementary classrooms. Students took on the role of note takers and researchers as they imagined they were traveling with Gulliver into a land of giants. The article describes how students used information in the story to find the scale factor, used measurement to enrich descriptions, made comparisons to develop a concrete picture, and created and described scale drawings.

Short, K.G., & Armstrong, J. (1993). Moving toward inquiry: Integrating literature into the science curriculum. *The New Advocate, 6*(3), 183–199.

> A university researcher, teacher researcher, and group of 2nd grade students collaborated in using inquiry to learn about cycles and ecosystems. They examined the role of literature in an inquiry cycle framework for curriculum and described the problems they encountered in moving toward greater use of discussion and content area inquiry in the classroom.

Other Articles

Copenhaver, J. (1993). Instances of inquiry. *Primary Voices K–6, 1*(1), 6–13.

Ernst, K. (1993). Carl creating: Going inside pictures and words in an artist's workshop. *Teacher Research: The Journal of Classroom Inquiry, 1*(1), 37–48.

Glover, M.K. (1990). A bag of hair: American 1st graders experience Japan. *Childhood Education, 66*(3), 155–159.

Grant, R., Guthrie, J., Bennett, L., Rice, M., & McGough, K. (1993/1994). Developing engaged readers through concept-oriented instruction. *The Reading Teacher, 47*(4), 338–340.

Guzzetti, B.J., Kowalinski, B.J., & McGowan, T. (1992). Using a literature-based approach to teaching social studies. *Journal of Reading, 36*(2), 114–122.

Smith, J.A. (1993). Content learning: A third reason for using literature in teaching reading. *Reading Research and Instruction, 32*(3), 64–71.

Dissertation

Austin, S.R. (1989). *A field study assessing the role of children's literature in linking language arts, social studies and science as interdisciplinary units at the third and fourth-grade levels.* Unpublished doctoral dissertation, University of Pennsylvania, Philadelphia. (*Dissertation Abstracts International–A*, 50/09, p. 2782)

Teachers' Beliefs and Practices

Books

McConaghy, J. (1990). *Children learning through literature.* Portsmouth, NH: Heinemann.

> McConaghy, a teacher researcher, describes her own classroom practice of teaching reading and writing through children's literature. She shares her journey of becoming a lifelong learner with her students by providing examples from her own reflections and student writing samples and by suggesting ways for others to incorporate literature into their own classrooms.

White, C. (1990). *Jevon doesn't sit at the back anymore.* Ontario, Canada: Scholastic.

> White, a teacher researcher, describes her experiences of becoming a learner with her students, most particularly with one student, Jevon. As she collected data through journal notes, audio- and videotapes, writing samples, and photos, she began to put together a description of Jevon and his literacy experiences from the "story corner." Ultimately, she discovered that Jevon became her teacher, leading her to explore her own beliefs about teaching and learning.

Articles with Annotations

Canterford, B.N. (1991). The "new" teacher: Participant and facilitator. *Language Arts, 68*(4), 286–291.

> Canterford, a teacher researcher, portrays how her students responded to reading and her new role as a participant and facilitator during literature discussions. Through the use of audiotaped discussions, her journals, and meetings with a mentor, this action research documents both Canterford's transition and her students' acceptance of this new role.

Jipson, J., & Paley, N. (1991). The selective tradition in teachers' choice of children's literature: Does it exist in the elementary classroom? *English Education, 23*(3), 148–159.

> Fifty-five teachers from Massachusetts, Oregon, and Wisconsin responded to a questionnaire that focused on the criteria used in the selection of books for use in the classroom. The researchers concluded that the teachers' choices were based on curricular needs. The results also indicated an "unconscious gender and racial bias in teachers' assumptions of what is appropriate for kids to read."

Scharer, P.L. (1992). Teachers in transition: An exploration of changes in teachers and classrooms during implementation of literature-based reading instruction. *Research in the Teaching of English, 26*(4), 408–445.

> Scharer describes the changes of five teachers and their classrooms during a transition from basal reading instruction to literature-based instruction. Through the use of interviews, discussions, and classroom observations, she documents three recurring trends: patterns of support, patterns of difficulties, and patterns of change that were associated with these five teachers' ongoing transitions.

Zancanella, D. (1991). Teachers reading/readers teaching: Five teachers' personal approaches to literature and their teaching of literature. *Research in the Teaching of English, 25*(1), 5–32.

> This case study depicts five junior high teachers' personal approaches to literature, their attitudes and beliefs about teaching literature, and their individual teaching methods. Through interviews with these teachers and their students, nonparticipant observations, the teachers' written reactions to specific literature, and artifacts, Zancanella portrays the connections and conflicts these teachers experience between their own views and enactment in the classroom.

Zarrillo, J. (1989). Teachers' interpretations of literature-based reading. *The Reading Teacher, 43*(1), 22–28.

> This study is based on the case studies of 15 elementary teachers, and it details three distinct interpretations these teachers held toward literature-based reading: (1) core books, (2) the literature unit, and (3) self-selection and self-pacing. Zarillo discusses the teachers' common elements of success and suggests a combination of the three interpretations in developing a literature-based reading program.

Other Articles

Blass, R.J., Jurenka, N.E.A. (1990). The use of children's literature in the classroom. *Journal of Clinical Reading: Research and Programs, 3*(2), 5–8.

Brown, R., & Coy-Ogan, L. (1993). The evolution of transactional strategies instruction in one teacher's classroom. *The Elementary School Journal, 94*(2), 221–233.

Edelsky, C., Draper, K., & Smith, K. (1983). Hookin' 'em in at the start of school in a 'whole language' classroom. *Anthropology & Education Quarterly, 14*(4), 257–281.

Hancock, J. (1993). Sow a thought, reap an action. In L. Patterson, C.M. Santa, K.G. Short, & K. Smith (Eds.), *Teachers are researchers: Reflection and action.* (pp. 71–85). Newark, DE: International Reading Association.

Hess, M.L. (1993). "Why do I have to read?": Multiplying perspectives through peer response. *English Education, 25*(3), 148–156.

Levande, D.I. (1989). Teacher-reported factors influencing reading instruction. *Reading Improvement, 28*(3), 2–9.

Luke, A., Cooke, J., & Luke, C. (1986). The selective tradition in action: Gender bias in student teachers' selections of children's literature. *English Education, 18*(4), 209–218.

Martinez, M.G., & Teale, W.H. (1993). Teacher storybook reading style: A comparison of six teachers. *Research in the Teaching of English, 27*(2), 175–199.

Mills, H., & Clyde, J.A. (1991). Children's success as readers and writers: It's the teacher's beliefs that make the difference. *Young Children, 46*(2), 54–57.

Pace, G. (1991). When teachers use literature for literacy instruction: Ways that constrain, ways that free. *Language Arts, 68*(1), 12–25.

Pappas, C.C., Oyler, C., Barry, A., & Rassel, M. (1993). Focus on research: Collaborating with teachers developing integrated language arts programs in urban schools. *Language Arts, 70*(4), 297–303.

Poole, R. (1986). The books teachers use. *Children's Literature in Education, 17*(3), 159–181.

Scharer, P.L., & Detwiler, D.B. (1992). Changing as teacher: Perils and possibilities of literature-based language arts instruction. *Language Arts, 69*(3), 186–192.

Scharer, P.L., Freeman, E., Lehman, B., & Allen, V. (1993). Literacy and literature in elementary classrooms: Teachers' beliefs and practices. In D.J. Leu & C.K. Kinzer (Eds.), *Examining central issues in literacy research, theory, and practice* (42nd yearbook of the National Reading Conference, pp. 359–366). Chicago, IL: National Reading Conference.

Stewig, J.W. (1993). Self-reports compared with observer reports: Elementary teachers' uses of literature. *Reading Improvement, 30*(2), 86–92.

Sumara, D., & Laurie, W. (1991). The teacher's role in whole language. *Language Arts, 68*(4), 276–285.

Dissertations

Cerra, K.K. (1990). *Intellectual freedom and the use of books in the elementary school: Perceptions of teachers.* Unpublished doctoral dissertation, University of Minnesota, Minneapolis. (*Dissertation Abstracts International*–A, 51/06, p. 1905)

Frye, B.J. (1990). *Motivating intermediate grade students to read: An ethnographic study of four successful teachers and their classrooms*. Unpublished doctoral dissertation, University of Minnesota, Minneapolis. (*Dissertation Abstracts International*–A 51/08, p. 2665)

Hart, P.M. (1989). *Using developmental instruction in a preservice teacher education course: A quasi-experimental study*. Unpublished doctoral dissertation, Ohio State University, Columbus. (*Dissertation Abstracts International*–A 51/04, p. 1201)

Scharer, P.L. (1990). *Teachers in transition: A multiple case study of teachers increasing the use of literature for reading instruction*. Unpublished doctoral dissertation, Ohio State University, Columbus. (*Dissertation Abstracts International*–A 51/12, p. 4076)

Walworth, M.E. (1990). *Second grade pupils' and teachers' expressed perceptions of text and illustrations in selected picture books*. Unpublished doctoral dissertation, University of Georgia, Athens. (*Dissertation Abstracts International*–A 52/06, p. 2090)

Instructional Strategies

Within the classroom curriculum, teachers and students may select from a wide range of possible engagements with literature. Some of these choices immerse students in voluntary reading and read-alouds. These experiences support students' development as proficient readers with a broad knowledge of literature. Other engagements with literature occur within the context of instructional lessons in which students work at developing more effective and efficient reading strategies. Shared reading immerses students in wide reading and then later focuses their attention on learning about language. Still other engagements involve readers in an in-depth, critical consideration of meaning through discussion, written response, art, or drama.

Some of the research studies included in this section look at the effectiveness of a particular instructional strategy that involves literature. Others examine a set of strategies that have been combined into a broader instructional unit. While these strategies are often part of the literature-based programs described in other research studies, the focus in this research is not on describing a broad program but on researching the effectiveness of a specific instructional strategy. Sometimes these instructional strategies are studied within literature-based classrooms, and other times the strategies are studied in isolation within a basal reader curriculum.

The subcategories in this section are read-aloud, voluntary reading, other instructional strategies, and technology. Instructional strategies that highlight response to literature are located in the reader response section.

Read-Aloud Research

These studies examine the effect of teachers reading aloud to school-age children as well as how teachers and students select books for reading aloud. This research area has a long tradition of studies detailing the many positive effects of reading aloud to children of all ages. Most of the research focuses on the reading aloud of fiction to children, although several studies look at poetry.

Most of the articles on read-aloud were found in reading education journals, and a few were obtained from English education journals. None, however, were located in library science journals. Often the individuals who publish research in this area are associated with colleges or universities as faculty members or graduate students in education. Several of the research studies were written by teacher researchers.

Elementary students were participants in most of the studies, with more studies conducted with primary grades (ages 5–9) than intermediate grades (ages 10–12). No research articles or dissertations were found that focus on middle school students and the read-aloud process. Additional research involving read-aloud experiences with young children can be found in the section on Family and Preschool Literacy.

Several methods were used to gather the research data. In a few studies, survey methods were used to determine teachers' and students' preferences for read-aloud. Other studies used qualitative methods to gather children's oral and written responses to literature and to observe teacher attitudes and use of read-aloud time. Much of this research has focused on the effects of reading aloud on children's vocabulary and written composition skills.

There are many possibilities for future research in read-aloud. Additional research studies being conducted and published by teacher researchers would be useful to educators at all levels. Such studies would provide more long-term and contextually-based data on the read-aloud process. Current research has primarily focused on children's responses to read-aloud through talk and writing. Further research examining children's responses to read-aloud through drama, art, or music could provide additional insights about the effects of read-aloud on children's understandings. More research needs to be done on children reading aloud to their classmates and on individuals other than classroom teachers who read aloud to children. School librarians make extensive use of read-aloud in their library programs; however, there is an absence of research in this area. Research on the read-aloud experience in middle schools could provide support for the importance of reading aloud to children of all ages. There are the many different uses of read-aloud experiences that are reflected in descriptions of literature-based classrooms, but they do not seem to be reflected in the research.

Review of Research

Hoffman, J.V., Roser, N.L., & Battle, J. (1993). Reading aloud in the classroom: From the modal toward a "model". *The Reading Teacher, 46*(6), 496–503.

> This review reports on read-aloud research and includes studies of classrooms from prekindergarten to 6th grade. The research encourages teachers to have a model story time so read-aloud experiences can be maximized. Also suggested is the need to provide sufficient resources and instruction for teachers.

Articles with Annotations

Dressel, J.H. (1990). The effects of listening to and discussing different qualities of children's literature on the narrative writing of fifth graders. *Research in the Teaching of English, 24*(4), 397–414.

This study examined whether the quality of literature that was read aloud to and discussed by 5th graders of different reading abilities would affect their writing. The students were randomly assigned to hear either high or lower quality detective stories and to write their own original detective stories. The stories written by children who heard and discussed high quality literature were rated higher in literary quality and genre development than were stories written by children who heard and discussed lesser quality literature.

Feitelson, D., Kita, B., & Goldstein, Z. (1986). Effects of listening to series stories on first graders' comprehension and use of language. *Research in the Teaching of English*, *20*(4), 339–356.

Experimental and control classes were randomly selected from a school in Israel to examine the effects of reading series-format stories to disadvantaged 1st graders. Children in the control classes continued their usual activities, including reading and writing, while the experimental classes were read to for 20 minutes over 6 months. The children who were read to outscored their counterparts on various comprehension and language measures.

Lenz, L. (1992). Crossroads of literacy and orality: Reading poetry aloud. *Language Arts*, *69*(8), 597–603.

Second graders were immersed in poetry during this 2-year study. The students spent time reading poetry and developing techniques for presenting poems to their class. The teacher-researcher argues that there is a bridge between orality and literacy that is too often overlooked.

Smith, N.J., Greenlaw, M.J., & Scott, C.J. (1987). Making the literate environment equitable. *The Reading Teacher*, *40*(4), 400–407.

In a survey 254 elementary teachers were asked to determine the book titles they prefer for read-aloud. Teachers selected books with a male protagonist most frequently. Books that included minorities, the elderly, and the physically or mentally challenged were often omitted for read-aloud purposes. The researchers suggest that teachers should actively and consciously select books that represent a more balanced view of sex roles.

Other Articles

Hoffman, J.V., Roser, N.L., & Farest, C. (1988). Literature-sharing strategies in classrooms serving students from economically disadvantaged and language different home environments. In J.E. Readence & S.R. Baldwin (Eds.), *Literacy research, theory, and practice: Views from many perspectives* (41st yearbook of the National Reading Conference, pp. 331–337). Chicago, IL: National Reading Conference.

Hoffman, J.V., Roser, N.L., Battle, J., Farest, C., Myers, P., & Labbo, L. (1991). Evaluating the effects of a read-aloud/response program. In J. Zutell & S. McCormick (Eds.), *Learner factors/teacher factors: Issues in literacy research and instruction* (40th yearbook of the National Reading Conference, pp. 297–303). Chicago, IL: National Reading Conference.

Leung, C.B. (1992). Effects of word-related variables on vocabulary growth through repeated read-aloud events. In C.K. Kinzer & D.J. Leu (Eds.), *Literacy research, theory and practice: Views from many perspectives* (41st yearbook of the National Reading Conference, pp. 491–498). Chicago, IL: National Reading Conference.

McKay, G. (1986). Poetry and the young child. *English in Australia, 76,* 52–58.

Mendoza, A. (1985). Reading to children: Their preferences. *The Reading Teacher, 38*(6), 522–527.

Michener, D.M. (1989). Reading aloud to students and written composition skills: Assessing their relationship. *English Quarterly, 21*(4), 212–223.

Morrow, L. (1988). Young children's responses to one-to-one story readings in school settings. *Reading Research Quarterly, 23*(1), 89–107.

Morrow, L.M., & Smith, J.K. (1990). The effects of group size on interactive storybook reading. *Reading Research Quarterly, 25*(3), 213–231.

Myers, P. (1990). Stories from print. *Language Arts, 67*(8), 824–831.

Nicholson, T., & Whyte, B. (1992). Matthew effects in learning new words while listening to stories. In C.K. Kinzer & D.J. Leu (Eds.), *Literacy research, theory and practice: Views from many perspectives* (41st yearbook of the National Reading Conference, pp. 499–503). Chicago, IL: National Reading Conference.

Roser, N. (1987). Research currents: Rethinking literature and literacy. *Language Arts, 64*(1), 90–97.

Sullivan, J. (1987). Read aloud sessions: Tackling sensitive issues through literature. *The Reading Teacher, 40*(9), 874–878.

Dissertations

Cosgrove, M.S. (1987). *Reading aloud to children: The effects of listening on the reading comprehension and attitudes of fourth and sixth graders in six communities in Connecticut.* Unpublished doctoral dissertation, University of Connecticut, Storrs. (*Dissertation Abstracts International–A*, 48/07, p. 1638)

O'Connor, E.M. (1989). *The effect of story reading as an instructional strategy of kindergarten children's literacy skill development.* Unpublished doctoral dissertation, Rutgers University, New Brunswick, NJ. (*Dissertation Abstracts International*–A, 51/02, p. 466)

O'Rourke, A.B. (1990). *Reading aloud to students as a classroom practice in kindergarten through grade six: A census of four school districts.* Unpublished doctoral dissertation, Harvard University, Cambridge, MA. (*Dissertation Abstracts International*–A, 51/06, p. 1970)

Voluntary Reading

Voluntary reading highlights personal choice, reading widely from a variety of literature, and the value of having students choose what and when to read. Research in voluntary reading spans all ages and looks at student choice during instructional hours at school and leisure reading in the home. As with read-aloud research, studies on voluntary reading have a long research tradition that indicates their positive effects on children's development as proficient readers. Much of the voluntary reading research applies insights from research on reading attitudes and interests to instructional contexts and strategies.

These studies are generally located in education and reading research journals. The research methods are often based on surveys and interviews and usually involve some kind of counting of books and children. Student self-reporting is a dominant, though usually problematic, methodology. Data collected in this way is not always reliable, and some researchers have resorted to offering rewards to students in order to maintain their interest over the course of the study.

Research in voluntary reading has established a positive relationship between the amount of reading and reading achievement. It also indicates that self-selection of materials promotes a more positive attitude about reading. The movement toward a "Sustained Silent Reading" time in the classroom indicates that teachers are recognizing the value of giving students time to read books of their own choosing without interruption.

The studies also provide evidence that very little reading is done at home and that students are not receiving adequate classroom instruction on how to self-select books for independent reading. The research demonstrates that students have difficulty choosing books at the appropriate reading proficiency level that are of interest to them and that they receive little or no assistance in making these choices. Children from classrooms that use a literature approach or have appealing classroom libraries seem to become more proficient readers with more positive attitudes about reading than children from classrooms without this emphasis. It is evident that such an approach results in more time spent reading in the home.

Research on teacher beliefs and behaviors regarding voluntary reading suggests that teachers may lack knowledge about the field of current children's literature. Teachers need to develop new understanding about how children's literature can be used throughout the curriculum so it becomes relevant to students. Teachers should be responsible for teaching the necessary reading skills as well as for encouraging voluntary reading to develop lifelong readers.

Missing from this field of research are long-term ethnographic studies. Case studies that extend over time in homes and classrooms and use field notes and anecdotal records could examine what students are really doing when they have time to read and can self-select reading materials. One researcher points out that continued research is needed so that teachers will see the importance of voluntary reading and devote more instructional time to it. Because proficiency in reading does not ensure that a student will read widely, this field of research may also need to identify further strategies for supporting students in self-selection of reading material. Studies about home and school cooperation may show additional ways to support children so they will not only know how to read but will choose to read throughout their lifetime.

Reviews of Research

Lesesne, T. (1991). Developing lifetime readers: Suggestions from fifty years of research. *English Journal, 80*(6), 61–63.

> This review offers five suggestions for developing a life-long love of reading in upper level students. Each key point is stressed, and relevant studies and articles are cited.

Morrow, L.M. (1991). Promoting voluntary reading. In J. Flood, J. Jensen, D. Lapp, & J. Squire (Eds.), *Handbook of research on teaching the English language arts.* New York: Macmillan.

> This chapter reviews the professional literature concerning the promotion of voluntary reading and provides a statement of its significance and a rationale for its greater role in the instructional program. The research also describes successful programs in promoting voluntary reading. The review addresses the extent of voluntary reading, its benefits, the characteristics of voluntary readers and their homes, and the theoretical framework and strategies for promoting voluntary reading at school.

Articles with Annotations

Anderson, G., Higgins, D., and Wurster, S. (1985). Differences in the free-reading books selected by high, average, and low achievers. *The Reading Teacher, 39*(3), 326–330.

> In this study 4th and 6th graders in four Arizona elementary schools kept a free-reading log for 5 weeks. Findings concluded that easy-to-read books that are of

interest to children will be most successful in engaging students in reading. The researchers discuss why low achievers may not select books suitable for recreational reading, and they offer suggestions for helping children make good choices.

Anderson, R., Wilson, P., & Fielding, L. (1988). Growth in reading and how children spend their time outside of school. *Reading Research Quarterly, 23*(3), 285–303.

This study examines the amount of time spent in reading and reading achievement outside of school. On a daily basis, 155 students in grade 5 reported the number of minutes they spent on out-of-school activities. Researchers found that the amount of time spent reading books was the best predictor of a child's growth as a reader from 2nd to 5th grade. The study also notes that the teacher has a significant influence on the amount of book reading children do out of school.

Greaney, V., & Hegarty, M. (1987). Correlates of leisure-time reading. *Journal of Research in Reading, 10*(1), 3–20.

This study investigates how the variables of reading attitude, motivation for reading, and home environment affect leisure reading. Four classes of 5th graders participated. The results suggest that reading attitude correlates more highly with leisure reading than any of the other variables. The emphasis parents place on reading in the home, academic development, and intellect is seen to be of greater importance than other home considerations.

McIntyre, E. (1990). Young children's reading strategies as they read self-selected books in school. *Early Childhood Research Quarterly, 5*(2), 265–277.

The researchers conducted an ethnographic study of the strategies of 1st graders as they read self-selected texts in their whole language classroom. The children's reading strategies did not develop linearly but, rather, showed a general movement from a focus on pictures to a focus on print. Students often used a range of strategies that were influenced by the classroom learning environment.

Morrow, L.M., & Weinstein, C.S. (1986). Encouraging voluntary reading: The impact of a literature program on children's use of library centers. *Reading Research Quarterly, 21*(3), 303–336.

> The purpose of this study is to determine whether voluntary reading attitudes and behaviors in 2nd graders could be improved through the use of literature activities and classroom libraries. One control group and two experimental groups were followed for a 10-week base period, followed by 9 weeks of intervention. Results show an increase in children choosing to read during free choice time, even after the intervention ended. Girls were more responsive to the intervention than were boys.

Other Articles and Chapters

Christian-Smith, L.K. (1988). Girls' romance novel reading and what to do about it. *The New Advocate, 1*(3), 177–185.

Christian-Smith, L.K. (1989). Power, knowledge and curriculum: Constructing femininity in adolescent romance novels. In S. Castell, A. Luke, & C. Luke, *Language, authoring and criticism* (pp. 17–31). New York: Falmer.

Holt, S.B., & O'Tuel, F.S. (1990). The effect of sustained silent reading and writing on achievement and attitudes of seventh and eighth grade students reading two years below grade level. *Reading Improvement, 27*(4), 290–297.

Hiebert, E.H., Mervar, K.B., & Person, D. (1990). Research directions: Children's selection of trade books in libraries and classrooms. *Language Arts, 67*(11), 758–763.

Manning, G., & Manning, M. (1984). What models of recreational reading make a difference? *Reading World, 23*(4), 375–380.

Martinez, M., & Teale, W. (1988). Reading in a kindergarten classroom library. *The Reading Teacher, 41*(6), 568–572.

Morrow, L.M. (1987). Promoting inner city children's recreational reading. *The Reading Teacher*, *41*(3), 266–274.

Morrow, L.M. (1985). Attitudes of teachers, principals, and parents toward promoting voluntary reading in the elementary school. *Reading Research and Instruction*, *25*(2), 116–130.

Morrow, L.M. (1985). Field-based research on voluntary reading: A process for teachers' learning and change. *The Reading Teacher*, *39*(3), 331–337.

Neuman, S.B. (1986). The home environment and fifth grade students' leisure reading. *The Elementary School Journal*, *86*(3), 335–343.

Neuman, S.B., & Soundy, C. (1987). The effects of "storybook partnerships" on young children's conceptions of stories. In J. Readence & R.S. Baldwin (Eds.), *Research in literacy merging perspectives* (36th yearbook of the National Reading Conference, pp. 141–147). Rochester, NY: National Reading Conference.

Ohlhausen, M.M., & Jepsen, M. (1992). Lessons from Goldilocks: "Somebody's been choosing my books but I can make my own choices now!" *The New Advocate*, *5*(1), 31–46.

Smith, L.L., & Joyner, C.R. (1990). Comparing recreational reading levels with reading levels from an informal reading inventory. *Reading Horizons*, *30*(4), 293–299.

Swanton, S.I. (1984). Minds alive: What and why gifted students read for pleasure. *School Library Journal*, *30*(7), 99–102.

Taylor, B.M., Frye, B.J., & Maruyama, G.M. (1990). Time spent reading and reading growth. *American Educational Research Journal*, 27(2), 351–362.

Telfer, R.J., & Kann, R.S. (1984). Reading achievement, free reading, watching TV, and listening to music. *Journal of Reading*, 27(6), 536–539.

Dissertations

Brant, K.J. (1990). *The effect of recreational reading on emergent literacy of primary children.* Unpublished doctoral dissertation, Central Missouri State University, Warrensburg. (*Dissertation Abstracts International*–A, 51/06, p. 1966)

Gagne, K.D. (1992). *"Kids and Books": A model for television as a medium to lead children to literature.* Unpublished doctoral dissertation, University of Massachusetts, Amherst. (*Dissertation Abstracts International*–A, 53/02, p. 453)

Levine, D.M. (1987). *Jungian personality type and recreational reading patterns.* Unpublished doctoral dissertation, University of North Carolina, Chapel Hill. (*Dissertation Abstracts International*–B, 48/12, p. 3716)

Niemeyer, K. (1987). *Books and beyond: Reading achievement, reading for pleasure, and television viewing time.* Unpublished doctoral dissertation, Northern Arizona University, Flagstaff. (*Dissertation Abstracts International*–A, 49/02, p. 227)

Robinson, P.J. (1987). *An examination of teachers' utilization of sustained silent reading in elementaty school.* Unpublished doctoral dissertation, Boston College, Chestnut Hill, MA. (*Dissertation Abstracts International*–A, 49/02)

Thompson, L.W. (1992). *A study of low achieving students' recreational reading.* Unpublished doctoral dissertation, Indiana University, Bloomington. (*Dissertation Abstracts International*–A, 53/01, p. 113)

Other Instructional Strategies

The research here details a variety of instructional strategies used by teachers to support their students in making connections between literature and literacy. Many of these studies examine reading and writing connections in classrooms where children are part of both literature-based activities and writing engagements. Another group of studies looks at young children and the effect of such strategies as shared reading, repeated readings, and "pretend" reading on their growth as readers. The remaining studies focus on a range of instructional strategies including retellings, group work, reading workshop, drama, and the teaching of reading strategies and processes.

The methodologies used in these studies range from traditional experimental designs with treatment and control groups to case studies and long-term ethnographic research. Some examine the use of these strategies within literature-based classrooms so that the instruction is integrated into the existing curriculum. Others introduce an instructional strategy into a classroom curriculum as an isolated activity.

The area of instructional strategies has the potential for a great deal of future research. While there are many possible strategies to be examined, only, a relatively small number have been investigated, often with only one or two studies having been conducted on a particular strategy. Except for the studies of reading and writing relationships, much of the research in this subcategory examines the strategy over several days. Further classroom-based, long-term research on these strategies by classroom teachers and university educators will provide important data on the influence of these strategies on children's thinking and literacy. It may be that much of the long-term classroom research is currently focused on describing literature-based classrooms and programs rather than specific strategies within those programs.

Studies

Bearse, D.I. (1992). The fairy tale connection in children's stories: Cinderella meets Sleeping Beauty. *The Reading Teacher, 45*(9), 688–694.

> In this investigation a reading specialist looks at the ways in which 3rd graders connect their reading of fairy tales to their own writing of fairy tales. The researcher used both interviews and analysis of the written stories during her 6-week genre study. She concludes that students do make intertextual links and are able to draw on multiple texts and many different types of literary details and structures when they write their stories within a genre study.

Cairney, T. (1990). Intertextuality: Infectious echoes from the past. *The Reading Teacher, 43*(7), 478–483.

> This article reports on the first stage of a 2-year study of intertextuality that examines how the writing of 6- to 12-year-olds is influenced by previous textual experiences. Students in 6th grade were individually interviewed about the links between the stories they read and their writing. The results focus on the types of links they were able to identify and differences between high and low ability readers.

DuPont, J. (1992). The effectiveness of creative drama as an instructional strategy to enhance the reading comprehension skills of fifth-grade remedial readers. *Reading Research and Instruction, 31*(3), 41–52.

> The researcher measured the growth in reading comprehension skills of 5th grade remedial reading students after their exposure to a treatment of creative drama, which was integrated with children's literature. The children who received the drama treatment scored higher on a standardized test of reading comprehension than students who did not.

Pappas, C.C., & Brown, E. (1987). Young children learning story discourse: Three case studies. *The Elementary School Journal, 87*(4), 455–466.

> In three case studies, kindergarteners listened to the same story three times. After each reading, the children were asked to pretend read the story to the researcher. Students' understandings improved with each subsequent reading. The implication is that children need to hear good literature more than once so they can naturally discover story elements in context.

Sulzby, E., Branz, D.M., & Buhle, R. (1993). Repeated readings of literature and low socioeconomic status black kindergartners and first graders. *Reading & Writing Quarterly: Overcoming Learning Difficulties, 9*(2), 183–196.

> This article reports one part of a longitudinal study of the emergent literacy of both urban black kindergarteners and 1st graders of low socioeconomic status. In these classrooms, teachers were moving from a skills-based to literature-based curriculum. They were using practices such as repeated readings and were encouraging emergent literacy. Results indicated that these children have the same developmental patterns as other groups in proceeding toward conventional literacy and that children responded positively to changes in teacher instruction.

Swift, K. (1993). Try reading workshop in your classroom. *The Reading Teacher, 46*(5), 366–371.

> Swift conducted a teacher-research study in her 6th grade classroom to examine her reading workshop program. She describes the program and provides qualitative and quantitative methods of evaluation. Results show that this type of reading program has a positive impact on student attitudes and test scores.

Trachtenburg, P., & Ferruggia, A. (1989). Big books from little voices: Reaching high risk beginning readers. *The Reading Teacher, 42*(4), 284–289.

> First grade teachers used key elements from Lee and Allen's language experience approach, Samuel and Hold-

away's notion of the benefit of rereading, and Holdaway's belief in the benefit of using enlarged texts to devise their own natural approach to teaching reading. Students made gains in test scores and seemed to acquire a greater interest in books and in reading as a result of this methodology.

Other Studies

Barone, D. (1989). Young children's written responses to literature: The relationship between written response and orthographic knowledge. In S. McCormick & J. Zutell (Eds.), *Cognitive and social perspectives for literacy research and instruction* (38th yearbook of the National Reading Conference, pp. 371–379). Chicago, IL: National Reading Conference.

Barone, D., & Lowell, J. (1987). Bryan the brave: A second grader's growth as reader and writer. *Language Arts, 64*(5), 505–515.

Baumann, J., & Bergeron, B. (1993). Story map instruction using children's literature: Effects on first graders' comprehension of central narrative elements. *Journal of Reading Behavior, 25*(4), 407–437.

Block, C.C. (1993). Strategy instruction in a literature-based reading program. *The Elementary School Journal, 94*(2), 139–151.

Blyden, A.E. (1988). Shared story reading for severely handicapped learners. *Reading Improvement, 25*(1), 67–70.

Cairney, T. (1992). Fostering and building students' intertextual histories. *Language Arts, 69*(7), 502–507.

Carger, C.L. (1993). Louie comes to life: Pretend reading with second language emergent readers. *Language Arts*, *70*(7), 542–547.

Combs, M. (1987). Modeling the reading process with enlarged texts. *The Reading Teacher*, *40*(4), 422–426.

Hansen, J. (1992). Literacy portfolios emerge. *The Reading Teacher*, *45*(5), 604–607.

Hubbard, R. (1993). Time will tell. *Language Arts*, *70*(7), 574–582.

Leland, C., & Fitzpatrick, R. (1993/1994). Cross-age interaction builds enthusiasm for reading and writing. *The Reading Teacher*, *47*(4), 292–301.

Martinez, M. (1993). Motivating dramatic story reenactments. *The Reading Teacher*, *46*(8), 682–688.

Morrow, L.M. (1985). Retelling stories: A strategy for improving young children's comprehension, concept of story structure, and oral language complexity. *The Elementary School Journal*, *85*(5), 647–661.

Nielsen, D.C. (1993). The effects of four models of group interaction with storybooks on the literacy growth of low-achieving kindergarten children. In D.J. Leu & C.K. Kinzer (Eds.), *Examining central issues in literacy research, theory, and practice* (42nd yearbook of the National Reading Conference, pp. 279–287). Chicago, IL: National Reading Conference.

Otto, B.W. (1993). Signs of emergent literacy among inner-city kindergarteners in a storybook reading program. *Reading & Writing Quarterly: Overcoming Learning Difficulties*, *9*(2), 151–162.

Pappas, C.C., & Brown, E. (1987). Learning to read by reading: Learning how to extend the functional potential of language. *Research in the Teaching of English, 21*(2), 160–177.

Reutzel, D.R., & Fawson, P. (1991). Literature webbing predictable books: A prediction strategy that helps below-average, first-grade readers. *Reading Research and Instruction, 30*(4), 20–29.

Schirmer, B.R., & Bond, W.L. (1990). Enhancing the hearing impaired child's knowledge of story structure to improve comprehension of narrative text. *Reading Improvement, 27*(4), 242–254.

Sipe, L.R. (1993). Using transformations of traditional stories: Making the reading-writing connection. *The Reading Teacher, 47*(1), 18–26.

Solsken, J.W. (1985). Authors of their own learning. *Language Arts, 62*(5), 491–499.

West, J., & Oldfather, P. (1993). On working together: An imaginary dialogue among real children. *Language Arts, 70*(5), 373–384.

Winship, M. (1993). Writing informational books in a first-grade classroom. *Primary Voices, 1*(1), 7–13.

Wishart, E. (1987). Textual cohesion and effective reading: A teaching strategy. *Reading, 21*(1), 30–42.

Dissertations

Burton, F. (1985). *The reading-writing connection: A one year teacher-as-researcher study of third-fourth grade writers and their literary experiences.* Unpublished doctoral dissertation, Ohio State University, Columbus. (*Dissertation Abstracts International*–A, 46/12, p. 3595)

Kinder, S. (1989). *Literature study groups: Effects on readers' proficiency, concepts of the reading process, and attitudes*. Unpublished doctoral dissertation, University of Missouri, Columbia. (*Dissertation Abstracts International*–A, 51/05, p. 1562)

Montiel, Y.D.L.T. (1992). *Spanish-speaking children's emergent literacy during first and second grades: Three case studies*. Unpublished doctoral dissertation, Arizona State University, Tempe. (*Dissertation Abstracts International*–A, 53/03, p. 712)

Moriarty, T.E.E. (1990). *Using children's literature: How literature-based writing influences the development of phonological awareness*. Unpublished doctoral dissertation, Oakland University, Rochester, MI. (*Dissertation Abstracts International*–A, 52/02, p. 487)

Technology

This research investigates the interaction between children and children's literature as represented through technological media. These studies trace the historical trends of research on the interactions of children with technology and television, particularly during the 1970s. Earlier research on television indicated a negative impact on the reading habits of children who spent time watching television. However, in recent years, this research has begun to examine the interactions in a new light, focusing on the effects of television and learning in relation to children's reading and children's literature. These newer studies indicate that media, specifically television, can help children's transactions with literature in meaningful and positive ways. While there are many studies of technology, only a few were located that related technology to children's literature. These studies primarily used some type of in-depth interview or observation of children interacting with the technology.

Reviews of Research

Johnson, R.T. (1990). The videobased setting as a context for learning story information. *Childhood Education, 66*(3), 168–171.

> This overview summarizes research on the instructional use of video-based technology and the role of the teacher in supporting student learning from technology. The importance of structured, adult-mediated video activities is particularly emphasized in enhancing children's ability to comprehend stories.

Kozma, R.B. (1991). Learning with media. *Review of Educational Research, 61*(2), 179–211.

> The theoretical and research literature on learning with books, television, computers, and multimedia environments is examined to show how media affects the learner's mental processing capabilities.

Article with Annotation

Choat, E., & Griffin, H. (1986). Young children, television & learning: Part II. Comparison of the effects of reading and storytelling by the teacher and television story viewing. *Journal of Educational Television, 12*(2), 91–104.

> Choat and Griffin investigate three areas in their study: comprehension of stories read and stories viewed, comprehension improvement by method of teaching, and children's views on stories read and stories viewed. In part, the results indicate that teachers need to be more aware of the use and content of both stories read and viewed, and that children prefer and give more details about stories viewed.

Other Articles

Cooper, M. (1984). Televised books and their effects on children's reading. *USE-of-English, 35*(2), 41–49.

Lancy, D.F., & Hayes, B.L. (1988). Interactive fiction and the reluctant reader. *English Journal, 77*(7), 42–46.

Dissertations

Kantar, M.J. (1990). *Children's responses to televised adaptations of literature.* Unpublished doctoral dissertation, University of Minnesota, Minneapolis. (*Dissertation Abstracts International*–A, 51/08, p. 2666)

Ross, E.M. (1990). *The use of computer-mediated reading as a tool for improving reading comprehension in second-grade readers.* Unpublished doctoral dissertation, Columbia University Teachers College, New York, NY. (*Dissertation Abstracts International*–A, 51/03, p. 826)

Reader Response Research

Recently, there has been a tremendous increase in research on children's responses to literature within particular contexts. This category of research is based in literary criticism and reader response theories. These theories represent a shift from the New Critics' view that the text, in and of itself, holds a specific meaning to be extracted by the reader. Instead, researchers are now concerned with how readers make meaning from their experiences with texts in particular contexts. Although reader response theories and research all focus in some way on the processes by which readers make meaning, they vary in the roles assigned to the reader, the text, and the social context within which the reader experiences a particular text.

Both interactive and transactive perspectives on the reading process are represented in these studies. Research based on interactive theories usually singles out the reader or text for analysis based on the assumption that the two are separate entities that interact in the reading process. Research based on transactive theories looks at the transaction between the reader and the text (often referred to as the potential text). Out of this transaction, meaning is created, and a new text is produced that goes beyond both the reader and the potential text. In addition, transactional theories vary according to whether they focus exclusively on the transaction of the reader and the text or also consider the influence of social and cultural contexts on the nature of the transaction.

The majority of research articles on reader response are published in educational journals from the fields of children's literature, reading, language arts, and English education. While much of the research is conducted by university faculty and graduate students, a growing number of studies are being done by teacher researchers. This research usually uses some type of qualitative research methodology to gather and analyze children's oral and written responses to literature.

Because of the large number of studies on reader response, this section is organized into four subcategories according to the major focus of the research: influence of text, reader characteristics, context and instructional strategies, and response processes.

Reviews of Research

Beach, R., & Hynds, S. (1990). Research on response to literature. In E. Farrell & J. Squire, *Transactions with literature* (pp. 453–489). Urbana, IL: National Council of Teachers of English.

> This extensive annotated bibliography lists research completed since 1970 on readers' response to literary text. The annotations are organized into reader variables (orientation, development, and gender), text variables, response processes (general, engagement, and interpretation), instruction, and research methodology. For research prior to 1970, readers are referred to *Literature and the Reader* by Alan Purves and Richard Beach (NCTE, 1972).

Galda, L. (1983). Research in response to literature. *Journal of Research and Development in Education, 16*(3), 1–7.

> This review of research examines seminal theoretical and empirical investigations of response to literature and addresses methodological problems. Studies are categorized according to several dimensions of reader, text, and context that affect response. Many of these investigations form the basis for current research.

Galda, L. (1988). Readers, texts and contexts: A response-based view of literature in the classroom. *The New Advocate, 1*(2), 92–102.

The author offers implications for classroom practice based on a review of theory and research on response to literature. The review and suggestions are organized around the factors of readers, texts, and contexts which constitute the complex process of responding to literature.

Martinez, M.G., & Roser, N.L. (1990). Children's responses to literature. In J. Flood, J.M. Jensen, D. Lapp, & J.R. Squire, *Handbook of research on teaching the English language arts* (pp. 643–654). New York: Macmillan.

The research reviewed in this chapter encompasses the range of methodologies used to describe children's various modes of response in diverse contexts. This article divides the review of research according to the focus of the research in terms of the reader, text, and context that constitute a reading transaction. It begins with a summary of the changes in perspectives on how children learn, what occurs during the reading act or event, and how research is conducted. Concluding sections concern considerations for the research community and implications for the community of practitioners.

Probst, R.E. (1990). Response to literature. In J. Flood, J.M. Jensen, D. Lapp, & J.R. Squire, *Handbook of research on teaching the English language arts* (pp. 655–663). New York: Macmillan.

Probst gives a brief historical sketch of the concept of reader response then describes the research on response in terms of analysis of response, categories of response, factors affecting response, reader characteristics, analysis of development, and analysis of interactions. Final comments discuss the value of response-based approaches to literature.

Books

Cooper, D.R. (Ed.). (1985). *Researching response to literature and the teaching of literature: Points of departure.* Norwood, NJ: Ablex.

This book offers varying viewpoints on three aspects of response research: (1) What do we study? (theoretical base), (2) How do we study? (methodology), and (3) the study of classroom literature instruction. In Part I, the authors differ on whether to study the personalities of individual readers and their responses or to look more closely at communities of readers. In Part II, the authors suggest such methodologies as surveys, interviews, discussion, guided or free response, content analysis of response protocols, analysis, and scoring of retellings. Part III carries the first two parts into the classroom, and the authors look at the implementation and evaluation of new programs.

Holland, K.E., Hungerford, R.A., & Ernst, S.B. (Eds.). (1993). *Journeying: Children responding to literature.* Portsmouth, NH: Heinemann.

This book is a collection of university and teacher explorations and research based on Louise Rosenblatt's transactional theory of reader response (see p. 196). The chapters cut across age levels to yield insights into how children create meaning from stories, how literacy skills are enhanced, and the role of teachers in facilitating students' responses. Various topics are included, such as response to different genres, processes of response, developmental characteristics, cultural responses, and teachers' influences. Educators in this volume have shared experiences that add to the research on response as well as contribute ideas about successful classroom practices for other teachers.

Lehr, S.S. (1991). *The child's developing sense of theme: Responses to literature.* New York: Teachers College Press.

Two studies conducted on young children's ability to identify and generate themes are discussed. For the first study, the author spent 3 months comparing students in basal programs with students in literature-based programs in kindergarten and 2nd and 4th grades. The author read aloud to small groups of two to five students, asked them to draw responses, then held individual interviews. The second study, spanning a 6-month period, involved only 4-year-olds and used essentially the same methodology as the first study. From both studies the author concludes that young children can talk about meaning in the books they hear and read if they are given enough time to formulate their thoughts, freedom to speak openly, and exposure to adults who provide a secure atmosphere.

Nelms, B.F. (Ed.). (1989). *Literature in the classroom: Readers, texts, and contexts.* Urbana, IL: National Council of Teachers of English.

This volume offers discussion about responding to literature in various contexts as experienced by 1st and 7th graders, high school students, college teachers, researchers, and theorists. An introductory chapter argues for the importance of reader response theory. The book also contains research studies and reflective pieces concerning student responses to literature, interpretive approaches to text, and social dimensions of literature. Theory and practice are integrated to support the use of response-based teaching.

Newkirk, T., with McClure, P. (1992). *Listening in: Children talk about books (and other things).* Portsmouth, NH: Heinemann.

Filled with transcripts of children's dialogue, *Listening in* reports on collaborative research in a 2nd grade classroom and examines children's "digressions" during their discussion about books. The authors explore the oral culture of children and its interaction with the adult culture of teachers.

Purves, A.C., & Beach, R. (1972). *Literature and the reader: Research in response to literature, reading interests, and the teaching of literature.* Urbana, IL: National Council of Teachers of English.

This book is divided into four sections and reviews research in the teaching of literature. The first three deal with studies of response to literature, reading interests, and the teaching of literature, and each section is followed by a bibliography of the relevant research in that area. The fourth section gives conclusions and implications for instruction and further research. Finally, the authors provide an appendix of summaries of significant studies.

Pierce, K.M., & Gilles, C.J. (Eds.). (1993). *Cycles of meaning: Exploring the potential of talk in learning communities*. Portsmouth, NH: Heinemann.

> Teacher and university researchers report on their studies about talk in the classroom. Their research is based on the writings of Douglas Barnes and focuses on issues such as the creation of collaborative communities, involvement in literature discussion, and the creation of concepts through talk.

Short, K.G., & Pierce, K.M. (Eds.). (1990). *Talking about books: Creating literate communities*. Portsmouth, NH: Heinemann.

> The chapters in this book are written by teacher researchers and university researchers about their studies of literature discussions in classrooms. The work is divided into three major sections: establishing a context for literate communities, organizing the classroom to support talk about literature, and making decisions about curriculum and learning.

Influence of Text

The role of the text in reader response has been the focus of numerous studies at all grade levels. This category is defined by those studies that investigate the influence of particular aspects of text—genre, theme, tone, character, culture and ethnicity, or illustration—on the meaning making process of the reader. Findings from these studies support the power of text to encourage aesthetic response, discussion, and critical thinking about readers' personal lives as well as the world in which they live.

The majority of these studies focus on elementary grade students. While middle school students were included in a few studies that spanned grade levels, only one Canadian study focused on the influence of text on middle school students. These studies primarily use qualitative, sometimes ethnographic, methodologies. Analysis of discussion transcripts is a primary source of data. These transcripts are usually small group discussions that take place during one session or over several days. Frequently, the groups are teacher led, although some researchers examine groups in which students take on the primary role in initiating discussion topics. These researchers find that student-initiated topics usually indicate the areas in which students feel the need to make meaning of their reading experiences. Written artifacts, such as journal entries, art and poetry, and field notes describing instructional and classroom contexts and events often support the research analysis.

Additional research examining the influence of text on reader response is needed to support many current educational goals. The significance of teachers' and students' choices of literature for classroom use can be supported by studies that focus on response to texts that are and are not culturally relevant to students' own backgrounds. Children are surrounded with vivid portrayals of news events in the media and with adult discussions on a variety of topics. Research supporting the use of literature that helps students develop an understanding of a particular sociopolitical topic is presently minimal. Such documented studies of students' responses could encourage teachers to bring multiple perspectives on difficult topics to the classroom through literature.

The role of historical fiction in understanding social studies is another area in need of research, as is the study of children's responses to poetry and its role in the classroom. Visual literacy is a relatively new concern for teachers. Research that focuses on student response to the wealth of illustrations in literature as well as book format can highlight the value of a reader's understanding of art as a sign system. These understandings are especially important as students respond to books in which both pictures and print are essential to the telling of the story. Middle school students and students of diverse learning and reading abilities constitute other populations for which more published research is needed.

Articles with Annotations

Anderson, D.D., & Many, J.E. (1992). An analysis of children's responses to storybook characters in non-traditional roles. *Reading Horizons, 33*(2), 95–107.

> In this study of response to story characters in nontraditional roles, participants were 154 students in 3rd grade from diverse cultural and SES backgrounds. The conclusions include the value of a personal, free response in which children relate the aspects of a story to their own lives but are not forced to make judgmental statements.

Kiefer, B. (1988). Picture books as context for literacy, aesthetic, and real world understandings. *Language Arts, 65*(3), 260–271.

> This researcher went into kindergarten through 4th grade classrooms to examine literary and aesthetic interactions with picture books, especially in relation to artists' styles. The findings show that children develop a growing awareness of the artists' choice of aesthetic factors used to express meaning. Literature-based classrooms produced responses and discourse of greater depth than traditional ones.

Leal, D. (1992). The nature of talk about three types of text during peer group discussions. *Journal of Reading Behavior, 24*(3), 313–338.

> This study investigates the responses of 1st, 3rd, and 5th graders to three types of text (a storybook, an information book, and an informational storybook). Conclusions focus on children's use of prior knowledge, greater interaction among older students with their peers, and the po-

tential of the informational storybook to elicit response and discussion.

West, J., Weaver, D., & Rowland R. (1992). Expectations and evocations: Encountering Columbus through literature. *The New Advocate, 5*(4), 247–263.

Two texts with alternative perspectives concerning Columbus were shared with 4th and 7th graders. Students were encouraged to respond aesthetically and discuss the varying perspectives. This aesthetic approach to literary texts that contain sociopolitical issues supports the need to present various perspectives to students. Through literature, the reader's expectations and beliefs can be challenged.

Other Articles

Grice, M.O., & Vaughn, C. (1992). Third graders respond to literature for and about Afro-Americans. *The Urban Review, 24*(2), 149–163.

Hade, D.D. (1988). Children, stories, and narrative transformations. *Research in the Teaching of English, 22*(3), 310–325.

Kiefer, B.Z. (1986). The child and the picture book: Creating live circuits. *Children's Literature Association Quarterly, 11*(2), 63–68.

Kiefer, B. (1991). Envisioning experience: The potential of picture books. *Publishing Research Quarterly, 7*(3), 63–74.

McMahon, S.I., Pardo, L.S., & Raphael, T.E. (1991). Bart: A case study of discourse about text. In J. Zutell & S.M. McCormick (Eds.), *Learner factors/teacher factors: Issues in literacy research and instruction* (40th yearbook of the National Reading Conference, pp. 285–295). Chicago, IL: National Reading Conference.

Pappas, C.C. (1993). Is narrative "primary"? Some insights from kindergarteners' pretend readings of stories and information books. *Journal of Reading Behavior*, *25*(1), 97–129.

Tomlinson, C.M., & Lynch-Brown, C. (1989). Adventuring with international literature: One teacher's experience. *The New Advocate*, *2*(3), 169–178.

Trousdale, A.M. (1989). Let the children tell us: The meanings of fairy tales for children. *The New Advocate*, *2*(1), 37–48.

Trousdale, A.M. (1989). Who's afraid of the big, bad wolf? *Children's Literature in Education*, *20*(2), 69–79.

Unsworth, L., & Williams, G. (1990). Big books or big basals? The significance of text form in constructing contexts for early literacy development through shared reading. *Australian Journal of Reading*, *13*(2), 100–111.

Dissertations

Downing, M. (1989). *Adolescents respond to nonfiction: Transactions with authors*. Unpublished doctoral dissertation, New York University, New York. (*Dissertation Abstracts International*–A, 50/09, p. 2847)

Klatt, B. (1992). *Elementary students' responses to the genre of biography and to "Lincoln: A Photobiography"*. Unpublished doctoral dissertation, Texas A&M University, College Station. (*Dissertation Abstracts International*–A, 53/06, p. 1854)

Ponder, J.M. (1992). *Fourth-grade children's thematic interpretations of literary works within the genres of fantasy, realistic fiction and folktale*. Unpublished doctoral dissertation, University of Georgia, Athens. (*Dissertation Abstracts International*–A, 53/09, p. 3156)

Seidenberg, Rita N. (1985). *Strategies of fourth-grade students in recalling and comprehending fables.* Unpublished doctoral dissertation, Fordham University, Bronx, NY. (*Dissertation Abstracts International*–A, 46/11, p. 3307)

Smolkin, L.B. (1989). *The neglected genre in children's literature: Children's interpretations of play scripts through speech act predictions and reader response modes.* Unpublished doctoral dissertation, University of Houston, TX. (*Dissertation Abstracts International*–A, 50/08, p. 2414)

Zipperer, F.J. (1985). *A descriptive study of selected fifth- and eighth-grade students' involvement with futuristic science fiction.* Unpublished doctoral dissertation, University of Georgia, Athens. (*Dissertation Abstracts International*–A, 47/01, p. 111)

Reader Characteristics

In this subcategory of reader response research, the studies are concerned primarily with the reader and how factors within the reader affect the reader's responses to literature. Among the factors considered in these studies are age, ethnicity, gender, and physical disabilities. Several of the studies match a defined reader characteristic, such as gender, with a text factor, such as genre. Another group of studies examines the aesthetic stance, in which the reader's attention is on the personal, lived-through experience, and the effect of that stance on their response processes.

Most of the studies are conducted with upper elementary students and use data collected through interviews and written responses. About half of the studies occur within the natural context of ongoing classroom environments and curricula. The remaining studies use materials and procedures unrelated to the classroom curriculum that are selected and brought into the school setting by the researcher.

Although studies that attempt to isolate one or two reader characteristics are informative, the factors identified in these studies do not reflect the complexity of readers' minds and lives. Future research should consider long-term, field-based research as one way to explore one child's or several children's responses over time and across a variety of reading experiences.

Long-term studies would allow for a more in-depth look at what these readers are bringing to the reading experience. This would seem to be an area where classroom teachers could conduct research, given the insights gained from being with the same children daily and having a teacher's access to a wide range of reading opportunities.

Book

Many, J., & Cox, C. (Eds.). (1992). *Reader stance and literary understanding: Exploring the theories, research, and practice*. Norwood, NJ: Ablex.

> The chapters in this book consider the influence that a reader's or teacher's stance, or approach to a text, has on the experience of the literary work. The contributors focus on the manner in which readers involve themselves in the literary experience or the necessity for detachment from that experience for critical analysis to occur. Theoretical perspectives, students' perspectives, and classroom interactions related to reader stance are considered.

Articles with Annotations

Altiere, J.L. (1993). African American stories and literary responses: Does a child's ethnicity affect the focus of a response? *Reading Horizons, 33*(3), 237–244.

> In this study, sixty 3rd grade students in three self-contained classrooms in a Southwestern urban school were read African American literature and asked to respond in writing. The data was analyzed for the com-

plexity of the students' aesthetic responses. The study determined that the responses of Caucasian and Hispanic students were not significantly different from those of African American children.

Galda, L. (1990). A longitudinal study of spectator stance as a function of age and genre. *Research in the Teaching of English, 24*(3), 261–278.

This study examines students' oral responses to realistic and fantasy novels by contemporary children's authors. Participants were 35 4th, 6th, and 8th graders across 2 years and 8 4th through 7th graders across 4 years. Students' evaluative responses moved from mainly categoric in the 4th grade to more analytic in the upper grades. Students responded to fantasy with more categoric evaluations and to realism with more analytic evaluations. Findings are discussed in terms of development, genre characteristics, and classroom contexts.

Hartmen, M., & Kretschmer, R.E. (1992). Talking and writing: Deaf teenagers reading *Sarah, Plain and Tall. Journal of Reading, 36*(3), 174–180.

This study was conducted by a teacher researcher in a self-contained classroom with a group of 14-year-old deaf girls. The study demonstrates the way meaning is created through small group discussion and journals. The researcher includes a discussion of the characteristics usually found in a reader who is deaf.

Many, J.E. (1991). The effects of stance and age level on children's literary responses. *The Journal of Reading Behavior, 23*(1), 61–85.

In this study, 43 4th graders, 47 6th graders, and 40 8th graders were read the same three short stories and were asked to complete written free responses to each. Responses were analyzed for reader stance and level of understanding. Results indicate that the use of an aesthetic stance, in which readers focused on the lived through experiences of the work, was associated with higher levels of personal understanding and that level of understanding increased with grade level.

Other Articles

Arizpe, E. (1993). Unraveling one reader's story: The case of Ariadne. *Journal of Reading, 36*(5), 356–330.

Barone, D. (1993). *The Butter Battle* book: Engaging children's thoughts of war. *Children's Literature in Education, 24*(2), 123–135.

Bunbury, R., & Tabbert R. (1989). A bicultural study of identification: Readers' responses to the ironic treatment of a national hero. *Children's Literature in Education, 20*(1), 25–35.

Cherland, M.R. (1992). Gendered Readings: Cultural restraints upon response to literature. *The New Advocate, 5*(3), 187–198.

Cox, C., & Many, J.E. (1992). Toward an understanding of the aesthetic response to literature. *Language Arts, 69*(1), 28–33.

Galda, L. (1982). Assuming the spectator stance: An examination of the responses of three young readers. *Research in the Teaching of English, 16*(1), 1–20.

Many, J.E. (1990). The effect of reader stance on students' personal understanding of literature. In J. Zutell & S. McCormick (Eds.), *Literacy theory and research: Analyses from multiple paradigms* (39th yearbook of the National Reading Conference, pp. 51–63). Chicago, IL: National Reading Conference.

Many, J.E. (1992). The effect of grade and stance on readers' intertextual and autobiographical responses to literature. *Reading Research and Instruction, 31*(4), 60–69.

Many, J.E. (1992). Living through literacy experiences versus literacy analysis: Examining stance in children's response to literature. *Reading Horizons, 32*(3), 169–183.

Marriot, S. (1985). "Me mum she says it's bigotry": Children's responses to The Twelfth Day of July. *Children's Literature in Education, 16*(1), 53–61.

Raphael, R., & Brock, C. (1993). Mei: The literacy culture in an urban elementary school. In D.J. Leu & C.K. Kinzer, *Examining central issues in literacy research, theory, and practice* (42nd yearbook of the National Reading Conference, pp. 179–188). Chicago, IL: National Reading Conference.

Dissertations

Carlisle, L.R. (1988). *Response to literature among first-grade students: Exploring the possibilities.* Unpublished doctoral dissertation, University of Massachusetts, Amherst. (*Dissertation Abstracts International*–A, 49/05, p. 1044)

Cherland, M. (1990). *Girls and reading: Children, culture, and literary experience.* Unpublished doctoral dissertation, Arizona State University, Tempe. (*Dissertation Abstracts International*–A, 52/01, p. 120)

Kemp, M.R. (1989). *A study of the influence of children's literature on the moral development of academically talented students.* Unpublished doctoral dissertation, Memphis State University, TN. (*Dissertation Abstracts International*–A, 50/07, p. 1919)

Lemley, P.A. (1993). *Deaf readers and engagement in the story world: A study of strategies and stances.* Unpublished doctoral dissertation, Ohio State University, Columbus. (*Dissertation Abstracts International*–A, 54/02, p. 484)

Many, J. (1989). *Age level differences in children's use of an aesthetic stance when responding to literature.* Unpublished doctoral dissertation, The Louisiana State University and Agricultural and Mechanical College, Baton Rouge. (*Dissertation Abstracts International*–A, 50/08, p. 2441)

Instructional Contexts and Strategies

The research in this area examines how teachers organize and structure classroom learning contexts and introduce instructional practices to encourage student response and meaning making. Most of the studies show the positive effects of the interaction among students in an atmosphere that respects the individual's aesthetic response. These findings support the theoretical framework that meaning is socially constructed. The strategies most often studied are dialogue journals, literature logs, and small group discussions.

The studies of instructional strategies are spread fairly evenly across kindergarten through sixth grade and are, for the most part, conducted within actual classroom contexts. Only one study addressed the impact of instructional strategies on the responses of second language learners. Middle school and students labeled "at risk" also have received limited attention.

The research methods most often used in this research are qualitative in nature. Data collection includes transcripts of discussions and interviews, written artifacts, and fieldnotes. These fieldnotes focus on classroom events such as teacher-led or student-led small group discussions, the exchange of dialogue journals, writing in literature logs, and the classroom talk that surrounds literature experiences.

A review of the studies in this section shows a need for additional research in several areas. Since literature is being used for instruction in more and more classrooms, studies that look at the link between literature and inquiry would offer a more complete understanding of the ways students use literature to build a world view. Research involving middle school students as participants would encourage teachers to use instructional practices that engage students in the use of literature in an integrated curriculum. Studies involving second language learners are also necessary to encourage changes in instruction from skill and drill to authentic language use. More teacher research and collaborative research at all levels and with all students is essential to a clear understanding of how various instructional strategies work in specific classroom settings.

Articles with Annotations

Alverman, D.E., & Olson, J.R. (1988). Discussing read-aloud fiction: One approach for motivating critical thinking. *Reading Horizons, 28*(4), 235–241.

> This article describes the use of Paula Danziger's *This Place Has No Atmosphere* as a read-aloud by a middle school teacher to motivate adolescents to think and respond critically. The teacher used webbing and role playing along with discussion to elicit responses about word play, point of view, and evaluation of the author's ability to relate to her audience. The teacher's success is attributed to her ability to pace the discussions, ask students to give reasons for their assertions, and encourage students to become personally involved in their decisions.

Dekker, M.M. (1991). Books, reading, and response: A teacher-reseacher tells a story. *The New Advocate, 4*(1), 37–46.

> Dekker conducted a teacher research study to look at the effectiveness of reading logs with 2nd and 3rd grade students. She instructed the students to write a log letter to both a friend and the teacher once a week telling what they liked about the self-selected texts and why. Responses fell into three categories: retelling, simple evaluation, and elaborate evaluation. Dekker found that demonstrating how to write in the log proved to be in-

hibiting. When she told the students to respond in any way that seemed appropriate, the responses became more varied and meaningful.

de la Luz Reyes, M. (1991). A process approach to literacy using dialogue journals and literature logs with second language learners. *Research in the Teaching of English*, *25*(3), 291–313.

> This study looks at the effectiveness of a process approach to literacy by examining the ability of 6th grade Hispanic bilingual students to construct meaning in dialogue journals and literature logs. The data analysis from the 10 case studies indicated the relative success of the interactive journal and the limited success of the literature log. The author suggests that appropriate social, cultural, and linguistic adaptations need to be made with second language learners. Because the school district in which the study was conducted mandates that responses be in English, the children's ability to use the literature log reflectively was hampered.

Five, C. (1986). Fifth graders respond to a changed reading program. *Harvard Educational Review*, *56*(4), 395–405.

> This teacher researcher describes how she created a reading program to give her 5th grade students time to make meaning through writing and talking about books. She notes the important elements of her approach and examines their responses to literature through talk, written letters, maps, and sketches.

Goatley, V.J., & Raphael, T.E. (1992). Non-traditional learners' written and dialogic responses to literature. In C.K. Kinzer & D.J. Leu (Eds.). *Literacy research, theory, and practice: Views from many perspectives* (41st Yearbook of the National Reading Conference, pp. 313–322). Chicago, IL: National Reading Conference.

> This study examines the responses of five ethnically diverse 3rd, 4th, and 5th grade special education students to a model of reading emphasizing literature-based in-

struction and student response groups. The students met twice a week with one of the researchers to participate in a book club, composed of reading, writing, discussion, and instruction. Students enjoyed and benefited from the program, as indicated by their discussions and responses over time.

Golden, J., Meiners, A., & Lewis, S. (1992). The growth of story meaning. *Language Arts, 69*(1), 22–27.

This study is set in the Southwest in a 2nd grade classroom of Native Americans and examines the growth of story meaning over time as children read and explored Maurice Sendak's *Where the Wild Things Are*. The story events included a read-aloud discussion, exploration of the character's personality, communication with the author, and the expression of personal meaning through art. The researchers discuss the importance of authentic text, alternative interpretations, personal meanings, social meaning, and the use of a variety of response processes.

Leal, D.J. (1993). The power of literary peer-group discussions: How children collaboratively negotiate meaning. *The Reading Teacher, 47*(2), 114–120.

The benefits of peer group discussions of literature were explored with nine small groups of students from 1st, 3rd, and 5th grades. The texts read included a storybook, an informational book, and an informational storybook. The benefits of the children's collaborative talks about these three types of texts included the groups becoming a catalyst for learning, establishing a platform for peer collaboration and tutoring, and providing an opportunity for exploratory talk with a real audience. Benefits for the teacher and the impact of text type are also discussed.

Many, J.E., & Wiseman, D.L. (1992). The effect of teaching approach on third-grade students' response to literature. *Journal of Reading Behavior, 24*(3), 265–287.

This study examines the effect of teaching approaches on 3rd grade students' responses to three picture books. The approaches examined were literary analysis, literary experience, and no discussion. The teaching approach affected the content of students' subsequent efferent and aesthetic responses, with students from the literary experience approach treating literature as an aesthetic experience rather than an object to study.

Zarrillo, J. (1991). Theory becomes practice: Aesthetic teaching with literature. *The New Advocate*, *4*(4), 221–234.

A model for aesthetic teaching developed by the researcher was implemented in a classroom of 29 4th graders in an attempt to translate Rosenblatt's theory (see p. 196) into instructional practice. This study supports the need for aesthetic teaching in all classrooms to realize the full potential of literature in the lives of students.

Other Articles and Chapters

Atwell, N. (1984). Writing and reading literature from the inside out. *Language Arts*, *61*(3), 240–252.

Au, K.H., & Scheu, J.A. (1989). Guiding students to interpret a novel. *The Reading Teacher*, *43*(3), 104–110.

Au, K.H. (1992). Constructing the theme of a story. *Language Arts*, *69*(2), 106–111.

Close, E.E. (1990). Seventh graders sharing literature: How did we get here? *Language Arts*, *67*(8), 817–823.

Close, E.E. (1992). Literature discussion: A classroom environment for thinking and sharing. *English Journal*, *81*(5), 65–71.

Cothern, N.B. (1993). "E.R.M.A.A." A strategy affirming the individuality of response. *Reading Research and Instruction*, *32*(4), 1–14.

Farest, C., & Miller, C. (1993). Children's insights into literature: Using dialogue journals to invite literary response. In

D.J. Leu & C.K. Kinzer (Eds.), *Examining central issues in literacy research, theory, and practice* (42nd yearbook of the National Reading Conference, pp. 271–278). Chicago, IL: National Reading Conference.

Feiertag, J., & Chernoff, L. (1987). Inferential thinking and self-esteem: Through the Junior Great Books program. *Childhood Education, 63*(4), 252–254.

Fiderer, A. (1993). Talking and thinking: Making what we read ours. In L. Patterson, C.M. Santa, K.G. Short, & K. Smith (Eds.), *Teachers are researchers: Reflection and action* (pp. 60–70). Newark, DE: International Reading Association.

Five, C. (1988). From workbook to workshop: Increasing children's involvement in the reading process. *The New Advocate, 1*(2), 103–113.

Gilles, C. (1989). Reading, writing, and talking: Using literature study groups. *English Journal, 78*(1), 38–41.

Gillespie, J.S. (1993). Buddy book journals: Responding to literature. *English Journal, 82*(6), 64–68.

Graves, D.H. (1989). Research currents: When children respond to fiction. *Language Arts, 66*(7), 776–783.

Hickman, J. (1981). A new perspective on response to literature: Research in an elementary school setting. *Research in the Teaching of English, 15*(4), 343–354.

Hill, S.E. (1985). Children's individual responses and literature conferences in the elementary school. *The Reading Teacher, 38*(4), 382–386.

Kelly, P. (1990). Guiding young students' response to literature. *The Reading Teacher, 43*(7), 464–470.

Kempe, A. (1993). No single meaning: Empowering students to construct socially critical reading of the text. *The Australian Journal of Language and Literacy, 16*(4), 307–321.

Knobel, M. (1993). Simon says see I say: Reader response and the teacher as meaning maker. *The Australian Journal of Language and Literacy, 16*(3), 295–306.

Latshaw, J.L.K. (1991). Middle grade students' responses to Canadian realistic fiction for young adults. *Canadian Journal of Education, 16*(2), 168–183.

Martinez, M., Roser, N.L., Hoffman, J.V., & Battle, J. (1992). Fostering better book discussions through response logs and a response framework: A case description. In C.K. Kinzer & D.J. Leu (Eds.), *Literary research, theory, and practice: Views from many perspectives* (41st yearbook of the National Reading Conference, pp. 303–311). Chicago, IL: National Reading Conference.

McCutchen, D., Laird, A., & Graves, J. (1993). Literature study groups with at-risk readers: Extending the grand conversation. *Reading Horizons, 33*(4), 313–328.

O'Brien, K.L. (1991). A look at one successful literature program. *The New Advocate, 4*(2), 113–123.

Raphael, T.E., McMahon, S.I., Goatley, V.J., Bentley, J.L., Boyd, F.B., Pardo, L.S., & Woodman, D.A. (1992). Research directions: Literature and discussion in the reading program. *Language Arts, 69*(1), 54–61.

Roser, N.L., & Hoffman, J.V. (1992). Language charts: A record of story time talk. *Language Arts, 69*(1), 44–52.

Tiballi, B., & Drake, L. (1993). Literature groups. A model of the transactional process. *Childhood Education, 69*(4), 221–224.

Wells, M.C. (1992/1993). At the junction of reading and writing: How dialogue journals contribute to students' reading development. *Journal of Reading, 36*(4), 294–302.

Wilhelm, J.D. (1992). Literary theorists, hear my cry! *English Journal, 81*(7), 50–56.

Wiseman, D.L., Many, J.E., & Altieri, J. (1992). Enabling complex aesthetic responses: An examination of three literary discussion approaches. In C.K. Kinzer & D.J. Leu (Eds.), *Literary research, theory, and practice: Views from many perspectives* (41st yearbook of the National Reading Conference pp. 283–290). Chicago, IL: National Reading Conference.

Dissertations

Daniel, P.L. (1991). *Reader responses in student-led literature study groups and teacher-led whole class literature study group.* Unpublished doctoral dissertation, University of Oklahoma, Norman. (*Dissertation Abstracts International–A*, 52/06, p. 2021)

Farnan, N.C. (1988). *Reading and responding: Effects of a prompted approach to literature.* Unpublished doctoral dissertation, Claremont Graduate School, CA, and San Diego State University, CA. (*Dissertation Abstracts International–A*, 49/11, p. 3316)

Hanssen, E. (1992). *Look who's talking: Adolescents discussing their reading and writing.* Unpublished doctoral dissertation, Indiana University, Bloomington. (*Dissertation Abstracts International–A*, 54/012, p. 115)

Hess, C.A. (1992). *A descriptive study of affective journal reader responses to quality literature in a multi-ability environment.* Unpublished doctoral dissertation, University of

South Dakota, Vermillion. (*Dissertation Abstracts International*–A, 53/08, p. 2752)

Kinder, S.J. (1989). *Literature study groups: Effects on readers' proficiency, concepts of the reading process, and attitudes.* Unpublished doctoral dissertation, University of Missouri, Columbia. (*Dissertation Abstracts International*–A, 51/05, p. 1562)

Lefever-Davis, S. (1992). *The effects of story structure and reader response questioning strategies on second graders' oral and written responses to literature.* Unpublished doctoral dissertation, Kansas State University, Manhattan. (*Dissertation Abstracts International*–A, 52/09, p. 3177)

McClure, A. (1985). *Children's responses to poetry in a supportive literary context.* Unpublished doctoral dissertation, Ohio State University, Columbus. (*Dissertation Abstracts International*–A, 46/09, p. 2603)

Olsen, M.O. (1991). *The effect of the reader response journal technique on reading comprehension, attitude toward reading and writing ability of sixth and eighth-graders.* Unpublished doctoral dissertation, University of Connecticut, Storrs. (*Dissertation Abstracts International*–A, 52/03, p. 864)

Young, E.R. (1991). *Can children be critics?: A participant observational study of children's responses to literature.* Unpublished doctoral dissertation, Claremont Graduate School, CA. (*Dissertation Abstracts International*–A, 52/03, p. 832)

Response Processes

The articles in this subcategory focus on the processes readers use to make meaning as they respond to literature. This is a particularly significant area of research, as it has an impact on current literacy and learning theory as well as reader response theory. At the foundation of these theories are the processes involved in the transaction between individuals and their world, whether it is a print experience or experiences in other sign systems. Educators will be able to better match schooling and literacy instruction with the ways people actually learn by understanding the processes readers use to make meaning.

Most of the process studies indicate that meaning making is a social process. Thus literature discussions in small groups enhance each student's ability to make meaningful connections with a text. Further evidence shows the importance of the links among all the language processes (reading, writing, speaking, listening, and thinking), as well as other sign systems such as art and music, in deriving meaning from a text. One study points out the importance of intertextuality in developing students' ability to make connections across texts and to their own lives, thus deepening and intensifying meaning making.

The studies in this section were conducted in classroom settings using qualitative data collection methods such as audio and video recording, fieldnotes, surveys, interviews, and written artifacts. The researchers analyzed the data to create categories to describe both the processes used by readers and the meanings derived from the processes. Several studies were done by teacher researchers or teachers in collaboration with university researchers. While the work conducted by university researchers will continue to be necessary and useful, more teacher research and collaborative research in this area would be helpful in providing immediate and powerful connections between research and classroom practice.

The majority of these studies has been conducted with students in the intermediate grade levels. More investigations of the processes used by young children would increase the knowledge base about response processes. Such research may help educators develop strategies that encourage children to become more aware of their natural processes for meaning making as they grow as readers.

Articles and Chapters with Annotations

Crowell, C.G. (1993). Living through war vicariously with literature. In L. Patterson, C.M. Santa, K.G. Short, & K. Smith (Eds.), *Teachers are researchers: Reflection and action*, (pp. 51–59). Newark, DE: International Reading Association.

> The teacher researcher used news of the Persian Gulf War to stimulate interest among her 3rd graders in a set of picture books on war and peace. A group of five boys and three girls chose to participate in this text set discussion. The author used transcriptions of the group's readings and discussions to examine the impact of literature on social studies learning and the effect of current events on children's understanding of historical fiction. She also looked at the connections children make between historical fiction and current events. The author concludes that the children made strong emotional connections by putting themselves into the stories and developed a new historical awareness from which to interpret current events such as the Persian Gulf War.

Eeds, M., & Wells, D. (1989). Grand conversations: An exploration of meaning construction in literature study groups. *Research in the Teaching of English, 23*(1), 4–29.

> This study investigated 5th and 6th grade literature study groups led by teachers in training during a 5-week period. Children chose a novel from a group of four offered and met in study groups with preservice teacher leaders who were encouraged to be participants. An analysis of the data revealed that children of varying abilities appeared to be capable of expressing construction of simple meaning, but altering it as alternatives were heard; sharing personal stories connected to the reading; predicting, hypothesizing, and confirming or disconfirming; and evaluating the text as literature.

Langer, J. (1990). Understanding literature. *Language Arts*, *67*(8), 812–816.

> The author looks at the meaning making process of 7th graders as they are involved in reading literature. The study promotes a process approach out of which the author identifies four stances used for interpretation: (1) being out and stepping in, (2) being in and moving through, (3) being in and stepping out, and (4) stepping out and objectifying the experience. Differences between reading for informative purposes and literary purposes are also addressed. Implications for instruction include questioning strategies called "thought tappers."

Nikola-Lisa, W. (1992). Read aloud, play a lot: Children's spontaneous response to literature. *The New Advocate*, *5*(3), 199–213.

> This study focuses on the relationship between the content of children's books and the amount and type of playful behavior children exhibit, both language and dramatic, in response to these texts. Three groups of children, kindergarten through 2nd grade, were read selected texts. Conclusions support both the strong link between children's reading experiences and the world of play and the need to provide ample activities for language expression.

Vine, H.A., Jr., & Faust, M.A. (1992/1993). Situating readers: A six part series. *English Journal*.

> Situating readers: Introduction and invitation, *81*(7), 62–67.
>
> Situating readers: Part two: Sensing the general situation, *81*(8), 28–30.
>
> Situating readers: Part three: Sensing the particular situation, *82*(1), 72–74.
>
> Situating readers: Part four: Sensing the voices in the situation, *82*(2), 78–80.
>
> Situating readers: Part five: What disempowers meaning making? *82*(3), 33–36.
>
> Situating readers: Part six: What empowers meaning making? *82*(4), 75–78.

This series of six articles describes the authors' research and invites classroom teachers to replicate it on a smaller scale in their own classrooms. The authors set forth the theoretical foundation for the study, their five questions, and the data collection methods. The original study involved 288 readers in four age categories (11–12, 14–15, 17–18, and 20–25) reading Adrien Stoutenberg's poem "Reel One." The authors gathered 50 responses in each grade level. The authors analyze the reading responses of an 11-year-old 6th grader and two 14-year-old 9th graders. The authors look at the traditional practice of abstracting a theme statement, which they contend limits students' meaning making, and at what empowers readers to give a text "life, value, and validity." A more complete report of this research is available in a book by Harold A. Vine and Mark A. Faust, *Situating Readers: Students Making Meaning of Literature*, published by the National Council of Teachers of English (1993).

Other Articles

Bartelo, D.M. (1990). The linkages across listening, speaking, reading, drawing, and writing. *Reading Improvement, 27*(3), 162–172.

Battle, J. (1993). Mexican-American bilingual kindergarteners' collaborations in meaning making. In D.J. Leu & C.K. Kinzer, *Examining central issues in literacy research, theory, and practice* (42nd yearbook of the National Reading Conference pp. 163–169). Chicago, IL: National Reading Conference.

Bloome, D., & Egan-Robertson, A. (1993). The social construction of intertextuality in classroom reading and writing lessons. *Reading Research Quarterly, 28*(4), 305–333.

Bodycott, P. (1987). Developing reader critics: Products of wholistic learning. *Australian Journal of Reading, 10*(3), 135–146.

Danielson, K.E. (1992). Learning about early writing from response to literature. *Language Arts, 69*(4), 274–279.

Danielson, K.E. (1992). Literature groups and literature logs: Responding to literature in a community of readers. *Reading Horizons, 32*(5), 372–382.

Golden, J. (1986). Story interpretation as a group process. *English Quarterly, 19*(4), 254–266.

Hancock, M.R. (1992). Literature response journals: Insights beyond the printed page. *Language Arts, 69*(1), 36–42.

Hancock, M. (1993). Exploring the meaning-making process through the content of literature response journals: A case study investigation. *Research in the Teaching of English, 27*(4), 335–368.

Jennings, C., & Terry, G. (1990). Children's stories: A natural path to teaching thinking. *Dimensions,* 18(2), 5–8.

Langer, J.A. (1990). The process of understanding: Reading for literary and informative purposes. *Research in the Teaching of English, 24*(3), 229–259.

Martin, T. (1985). Horizons, themes and protensions. *Reading, 19*(1), 13–19.

McGee, L.M. (1992). An exploration of meaning construction in first graders' grand conversations. In C.K. Kinzer & D.J. Leu (Eds.), *Literacy research, theory, and practice: Views from many perspectives* (41st yearbook of the National Reading Conference, pp. 177–186). Chicago, IL: National Reading Conference.

Short, K.G. (1992). Intertextuality: Searching for patterns that connect. In C.K. Kinzer & D.J. Leu (Eds.), *Literary research, theory, and practice: Views from many perspectives*

(41st yearbook of the National Reading Conference, pp. 187–197). Chicago, IL: National Reading Conference.

Dissertations

Edmiston, P.E. (1990). *The nature of engagement in reading: Profiles of three fifth-graders' engagement strategies and stances.* Unpublished doctoral dissertation, Ohio State University, Columbus. (*Dissertation Abstracts International*–A, 51/12, p. 4075)

Gilles, C. (1991). *Negotiating the meanings: The uses of talk in literature study groups by adolescents labeled learning disabled.* Unpublished doctoral dissertation, University of Missouri, Columbia. (*Dissertation Abstracts International*–A, 52/06, p. 2086)

Innes, M.C. (1993). *Six children's responses to literature.* Unpublished doctoral dissertation, University of Alberta, Canada. (*Dissertation Abstracts International*–A, 53/08, p. 2681)

McMahon, S.I. (1992). *Book club: A case study of a group of fifth-graders as they participate in a literature-based reading program.* Unpublished doctoral dissertation, Michigan State University, East Lansing. (*Dissertation Abstracts International*–A, 53/03, p. 763)

Mason, K.M. (1990). *Revision and reader response: A year-long study in an eighth-grade classroom.* Unpublished doctoral dissertation, University of Georgia, Athens. (*Dissertation Abstracts International*–A, 51/10, p. 3350)

Paille, E.W. (1991). *Interaction in reader response: A one-year study of fifth-graders' literature groups and dialogue journals.* Unpublished doctoral dissertation, University of Georgia, Athens. (*Dissertation Abstracts International*–A, 52-06, p. 2089)

Smith, K. (1993). *A descriptive analysis of the responses of six students and their teacher in literature study sessions*. Unpublished doctoral dissertation, Arizona State University, Tempe. (*Dissertation Abstracts International*–A, 54/03, p. 809)

Summary

In the area of reader response, the majority of research has focused on the significance of discussion, shared interpretations, response journals, and literature logs. Further study needs to focus on the responses of young children and middle school students as well as students with diverse cultural and language backgrounds. Research is needed with all ages on their responses to a greater range of types of literature, particularly informational books, and reading materials such as newspapers and magazines that are such an important part of readers' lives outside of the school context. Research on children's responses to picture books needs to take into account the integration of print, illustrations, and book format by readers to create meaning.

While research analyzing children's oral and written responses has been productive and should continue, researchers also need to examine children's responses through other sign systems, such as art and drama. The use of other sign systems is particularly important with young children, who often have difficulty using oral and written language to express their responses to literature. The current research emphasis on oral discussions and written responses may be leading researchers to underestimate the complexity and nature of young children's responses to literature.

Current reader response research has primarily focused on how children's responses to literature influence their literary understandings and reading strategies. Because literature is also used in classrooms as part of thematic units and inquiry studies, future research examining children's historical, sociocultural, political, mathematical, or scientific understandings could produce new insights about response processes and instructional strategies. Another important area of research is examining the process of intertextuality and strategies for encouraging students to make connections that broaden, deepen, and expand their learning.

Qualitative research by university researchers will continue to play a critical role in adding to the knowlege base on reader response. In addition, long-term studies of responses in classroom learning environments by teachers and collaborative teams of teacher researchers and university researchers will be essential to understanding the complexity of response processes and the learning environments which support them.

Review and Selection of Children's Literature

The review and selection of children's literature focuses primarily on studies of adults and the processes by which they evaluate literature as well as their criteria for selecting children's books to use in the classroom and for library acquisitions. These studies examine issues such as a book reviewer's knowledge about illustration media and techniques as well as the review of controversial books in major book review journals. Other studies include research that focuses on differences in the types of children's books circulated from the school and public libraries within the same community, the limited availability of Spanish language materials for children in most school and public libraries, and the role of the library within the school context.

Articles in this category are primarily found in library science journals. The researchers are associated with a university or college in the field of library science. The methodologies vary as to the topic of the research study, but the majority of the studies utilize a survey method.

The research on review and selection is especially important in children's literature because adults write, review, purchase, and select what will be used with children in the classroom or library. Purchase and use of literature is the responsibility of the classroom teacher and school librarian. Many times, librarians will use review sources that may or may not include reviews from individuals knowledgeable about text and illustrations in children's books. More studies that extend beyond the survey methodology need to be conducted in education and library science, because these are the individuals responsible for bringing literature to children in the school environment. Survey methodology is limiting in that responses are recorded by individuals in ways that do not allow for direct contact and conversation with those who respond. There is also a tendency to count books rather than observe the use of those books in actual classroom and library environments. Librarians and teachers researching their own processes in the selection and use of children's literature would provide information on the value of using literature in the classroom and library as well as focusing on the quality of literature that is currently being published and purchased for use with children.

Articles with Annotations

Schon, I., Hopkins, K.D., Main, I., & Hopkins, B.R. (1987). Books in Spanish for young readers in school and public libraries: A survey of practices and attitudes. *Library and Information Science Research*, *9*(1), 21–28.

> This study investigates librarians' attitudes and practices regarding the selection, acquisition, and use of books in Spanish for children and young adults in public and school libraries serving a significant number of Hispanics. A survey of 142 public and county librarians and 356 school librarians indicates that 75 percent of the librarians who responded spend less than 1 percent of their total book budget for the purchase of books in Spanish.

Harvey-Slager, N.D. (1992). Left out, way back, and catch-up: The positions played by women's biographies in four elementary schools. *Journal of Youth Services in Libraries*, *5*(4), 385–397.

> This study was conducted in four elementary schools, each serving kindergarten through 5th grade, and focuses on the collection of women's biographies in each school library. The results indicate that the collections were not gender balanced in proportion to the school population and that the biographies were generally not high in literary quality. The researcher also indicates that

there is a lack of well-written minority biographies being published.

Other Articles

Bushbin, O.M., & Steinfirst, S. (1989). Criticism of artwork in children's picture books: A content analysis. *Journal of Youth Services in Libraries, 2*(3), 256–266.

Craver, K.W. (1984). Book reviewers: An empirical portrait. *School Library Media Quarterly, 12*(5), 383–409.

Crow, S.R. (1986). The reviewing of controversial juvenile books: A study. *School Library Media Quarterly, 15*(2), 83–86.

Garland, K. (1989). Children's materials in the public library and the school library media center in the same community: A comparative study of use. *Library Quarterly, 59*(4), 326–338.

Hansen, J. (1993). Synergism of classroom and school libraries. *The New Advocate, 6*(3), 201–211.

Pottorff, D.D., & Olthof, K. (1993). Censorship of children's books on the rise: Schools need to be prepared. *Reading Improvement, 30*(2), 66–75.

Veeder, M.H. (1992). Journalistic reviewing and children's books: A personal and professional perspective. *The Lion and the Unicorn, 16*(1), 83–89.

Dissertations

Meacham, M.E. (1989). *The development of children's book reviewing in selected journals from 1924–1964.* Unpublished doctoral dissertation, Texas Woman's University, Denton. (*Dissertation Abstracts International*–A, 50/11, p. 3400)

Weedman, J.E. (1989). *Communication patterns among cultural gatekeepers: A sociometric analysis of interaction among editors, reviewers, and critics of children's literature.* Unpublished doctoral dissertation, University of Michigan, Ann Arbor. (*Dissertation Abstracts International–A*, 50/06, p. 1467)

Section II: Professional Journals

A wide range of journals is currently available to educators to meet their professional needs. In this section, three types of journals related to children's literature are highlighted. The first and largest group of journals are those that have regular features, articles, or reviews of children's literature and its use in the curriculum. Some of these journals primarily publish research and content analyses of children's literature, while others are book review journals. Still others focus on broad issues of curriculum or literacy but include features on children's literature. In the annotation for each journal, information is given about the major focus and audience for the journal, its professional association, the types of articles and features included, the frequency of publication, and an address for ordering the journal. When available, phone numbers are also included. A chart that summarizes the kinds of articles and features in these journals is also included. This chart can be used to locate journals that publish a particular kind of information or article, such as reviews of children's literature, themed bibliographies, ideas on ways to use literature in the classroom, or information on conferences and awards.

The second group of journals includes those in which we located a number of research studies on children's literature, even though this was not their major focus. Educators who are searching for studies about children's literature will find it beneficial to look at these journals. The annotations offer the same type of information found in the previous section. In addition, the addresses of the research centers focusing on literature and reading are included.

The third group is a list of all the journals we examined through hand searches. Many of these are annotated in the previous two sections. Journals that contained only a few studies for 1985–1993 were not annotated in either section.

Professional Journals Featuring Children's Literature

➤ *Appraisal*
This journal is published quarterly by the Children's Science Book Review Committee, whose members believe that science books deserve the same careful attention as literary works for children. Book reviews are written by children's librarians and subject specialists. Within each issue, single book reviews are arranged alphabetically by author, and series reviews are grouped at the end of the issue by series title. A rating is given by the reviewers at the left of each review to indicate the quality of the book.

  Order from: *Appraisal*
      605 Commonwealth Avenue
      Boston, MA 02215

➤ *Bookbird: World of Children's Books*
This quarterly journal of the International Board on Books for Young People is an international periodical on literature for children and young adults. Included are articles about books and authors from various countries as well as prize winning books and books recommended for translation. A change in format and size was introduced with the September 1993 issue, which is a themed issue on violence in children's books.

  Order from: Bookbird Subscriptions
      434 W. Downer Place
      Aurora, IL 60506
      708-892-7465

➤ *Booklist*

The American Library Association publishes this journal twice a month from September through June and monthly in July and August. Its purpose is to provide a guide to current print and nonprint materials for adults and children to be considered for purchase by small and medium-sized public libraries and school library media centers. A review in Booklist constitutes a recommendation for library purchase. A star beside a title indicates a work judged by a reviewer to be outstanding in its genre. Bibliographies on selected topics are also included in each issue.

> Order from: *Booklist*
> 434 W. Downer Place
> Aurora, IL 60506
> 708-892-7465

➤ *Book Links: Connecting books, libraries, and classrooms*

Published by Booklist Publications of the American Library Association, this bimonthly magazine is designed for teachers, librarians, booksellers, and other adults interested in connecting children with books. It provides annotated bibliographies on many topics and themes, essays linking books on a similar theme, retrospective reviews and other features targeted at educators of children from preschool through eighth grade.

> Order from: *Book Links*
> 434 W. Downer Place
> Aurora, IL 60506-9936
> 708-892-7465

➤ *The Book Report*

The articles in *The Book Report*, a bimonthly publication, focus on the operation of secondary school libraries. Reviews of books and other media for young adults are included along with articles about authors.

Order from: Linworth Publishing Inc.
480 E. Wilson Bridge Road, Suite I
Worthington, OH 43085-2372

➤ *The Bulletin of the Center for Children's Books* (BCCB)
This monthly bulletin is published by the Graduate School of Library and Information Science of the University of Illinois and the University of Illinois Press. Each issue critically reviews current books written for children and adolescents. Code symbols are used to indicate whether the book is recommended by the reviewer. The last section of the bulletin contains reviews of professional materials.
Order from: University of Illinois Press
Bulletin of the Center for Children's
Books
54 E. Gregory Drive
Champaign, IL 61820
217-333-8935

➤ *Canadian Children's Literature* (CCL)
This bilingual (French/English) journal is published quarterly and includes brief editorial introductions, literary essays, topical articles, research reviews, and children's book reviews. Recent themed issues have focused on censorship, analysis of the range of Canadian children's literature and a critical analysis of Canadian picture books. Academics, school and public librarians, teachers, and parents are the intended audience for this peer reviewed journal.
Order from: Canadian Children's Press
Canadian Children's Literature
Association
University of Guelph
Departments of English and French
Guelph, Ontario, N1G 2W1
519-824-4120, 3189

➤ *CBC Features*

Published twice a year, this newsletter of the Children's Book Council (CBC) is "devoted to a topic of interest to people working with books and children." The publication and information on the many Children's Book Council activities are available for a one-time fee. The newsletter contains lists of numerous free or inexpensive items from publishers, such as posters, bookmarks, activity kits and author brochures, as well as information about special events related to children's literature.

Order from: *CBC Features*
350 Scotland Road
Orange, NJ 07050
212-966-1990

➤ *Childhood Education*

This professional journal of the Association for Childhood Education International (ACEI) is published five times a year. It contains brief articles addressing issues of interest to educators of children from infancy through early adolescence. Included in each issue is an annotated list of 25 children's books. These books are compiled into the Bibliography of Books for Children, which is published every three years by ACEI. Audio-visual materials, software, and professional books are also reviewed.

Order from: Association for Childhood Education
International
11501 Georgia Avenue, Suite 315
Wheaton, MD 20902
301-942-2443
800-423-3563

➤ *Children's Literature*

This annual is published by the Modern Language Association Division on Children's Literature and the Children's Literature Association. The annuals are sometimes organized around a theme and are composed of editorial notes, literary essays, articles, professional book reviews, and lists of dissertations. The journal takes a critical literary perspective on modern and historical children's literature, addressing issues such as culture and gender. The audience for this journal includes scholars working in the areas of literary and cultural studies, educators, librarians, and authors and illustrators of children's literature.

Order Volumes   John C. Wandell
1–7 from: Children's Literature Foundation
                 Box 370
                 Windham Center, Connecticut 06280
Order current   Yale University Press
volumes from: 92A Yale Station
                 New Haven, Connecticut 06520
                 203-432-0940

➤ *Children's Literature Association Quarterly*

This quarterly journal is published by the Children's Literature Association, a nonprofit organization formed to encourage serious scholarship and research in children's literature, particularly in the areas of literary and cultural studies. Issues frequently focus on special topics such as mothers and daughters in children's literature. The contents of the journal span topics such as bibliographies, critical approaches, curriculum and instruction, literary theory, historical studies, illustration, and national and minority literature. In addition to articles, there are notices of awards, calls for proposals, and reviews of professional books on scholarship in children's literature. Each year one issue is devoted entirely to an extensive bibliography on current scholarship on children's literature. This issue includes annotations of books, articles and dissertations of note.

Order from: Children's Literature Association
           Box 138
           Battle Creek, MI 49016

➤ *Children's Literature in Education*
This international publication is published quarterly for a scholarly audience of researchers, librarians, teachers, students, writers, and others who are interested in prose and poetry for children and young adults. The majority of articles include content analyses of social issues, text and literary analyses, author and illustrator studies, and historical studies. Recent issues have included some applications of literature to classroom use as well as children's responses to literature. Occasionally reviews of professional books that critically analyze an author or genre are included.

> Order from: Subscription Department
> Human Sciences Press, Inc.
> 233 Spring Street
> New York, New York 10013-1578
> 212-807-1047

➤ *Dragon Lode*
Children's Literature and Reading, a special interest group of the International Reading Association, publishes this journal three times a year. The *Dragon Lode* prints brief articles on all facets of children's literature in the reading program. Each issue explores areas of concern to those interested in children's literature. Reviews of children's books are also included. Subscription cost includes membership in the group.

> Order from: Dr. Rosemary Salesi
> R.R. #2 Box 923
> Bangor, ME 04401
> or contact the International Reading
> Association.

➤ *English Journal*
This peer-reviewed journal is the secondary (grades 7–12) publication of the National Council of Teachers of English

(NCTE). It is published eight times a year and contains articles that focus primarily on issues involving literature and writing instruction. The articles range from descriptions of classroom practices to research studies and are primarily aimed at an audience of classroom teachers, teacher researchers, and teacher educators. Also published are reviews of professional books, letters and poetry submitted by readers, information on conferences and awards, and a column on books for teenage readers. The subscription cost includes membership in NCTE.

Order from: National Council of Teachers of English
1111 W. Kenyon Road
Urbana, IL 61801-1096
217-328-3870
800-369-6283

➤ *The Five Owls*
Published five times a year, this journal is intended for librarians, teachers, authors, illustrators, and other individuals interested in children's literature. The editors state that the journal "can be used as a guide to using literature in the curriculum, as a trusted selection tool, as a source of creative new ideas for your school or library, and as an enjoyable way to stay in touch with what is happening in children's books." Contains articles and bibliographies based on the issue's theme. Book reviews and interviews with authors are included.

Order from: *The Five Owls*
2004 Sheridan Avenue South
Minneapolis, MN 55405
612-377-2004

➤ *The Horn Book Magazine*
Published bimonthly, Horn Book reviews current children's books, which are classified by age level and subject. This

journal also provides articles on authors, illustrators, Caldecott and Newbery award winners, and other issues in children's literature. Frequently reviewed are books in Spanish and books that have been reissued or have recently been published in paperback form. A list of outstanding books is featured each year.

Order from: The Horn Book, Inc.
14 Beacon Street
Boston, MA 02108-9765
617-227-1555
800-325-1170

➤ *Journal of Children's Literature*
Formerly called *The Bulletin*, this refereed journal is published twice a year by the Children's Literature Assembly, an affiliate of the National Council of Teachers of English. The journal focuses on the art and study of teaching from elementary through college as it relates to children's literature. Issues are sometimes themed and include critical discussions of children's books, authors and illustrators, curricular materials, educational practices with children's literature, research, and current trends. Extended reviews of a single professional or children's book are included. The Fall issue contains that year's notable list of children's trade books in the language arts. The subscription cost is included in the membership fee.

Order from: Children's Literature Assembly
c/o Marjorie Hancock
2037 Plymouth Road
Manhattan, KS 66502

or contact the National Council of Teachers of English.

➤ *Journal of Reading*
This peer-reviewed journal is published eight times a year by the International Reading Association. The journal is written for those interested in the current research, prac-

tice, and theory concerning the teaching of reading to adolescents and adults. It includes information of professional value to educators and book reviews of both adolescent books and professional resources. An annotated list of books selected for the Young Adult Choices award is published in the November issue. A subscription includes membership in the International Reading Association.

Order from: International Reading Association
800 Barksdale Road
PO Box 8139
Newark, DE 19714-8139
302-731-1600
800-628-8508

➤ *Journal of Youth Services in Libraries*
This quarterly journal is published by the Association for Library Service to Children division of the American Library Association. Issues contain articles related to children's literature, library services, international publishing news, the May Hill Arbuthnot honor lecture, the Caldecott and Newbery award speeches, and other features. Subscription cost is included in the membership fee.

Order from: American Library Association
Association of Library Service
to Children
50 E. Huron Street
Chicago, IL 60611
800-545-2433

➤ *Kirkus Reviews*
Published semi-monthly, this journal contains reviews of books for adults and children as well as an index. The reviews of books for young children state the genre and format of the book as well as the suggested age of the child. Books of special note are indicated with a diamond.

Order from: Kirkus Reviews
200 Park Avenue South
New York, NY 10003

> *Kliatt*

Kliatt is published six times a year with an annual cumulative index in the November issue. This journal contains reviews of paperback books, audiobooks, and educational software recommended for libraries and classrooms serving young adults. A code is used to help readers determine if the material reviewed is appropriate for their needs. Brief articles of interest to those working with young adults begin each issue.

Order from: *Kliatt*
33 Bay State Road
Wellesley, MA 02181

> *Language Arts*

This peer-reviewed journal of the National Council of Teachers of English is published eight times a year. It covers all facets of language arts learning and teaching of interest to educators working with children from preschool to middle school. Each issue contains articles representing a particular theme such as literature-based language arts programs, spelling, and language arts for special populations. Articles on various aspects of children's literature and its use in the elementary curriculum frequently appear. The departments include bookalogues (reviews of recent children's books) and profiles of children's authors and illustrators. The October issue contains a notable children's book list for language arts.

Order from: National Council of Teachers of English
1111 W. Kenyon Road
Urbana, IL 61801-1096
217-328-3870
800-369-6283

➢ *Library Talk: The Magazine for Elementary School Librarians*

This journal contains articles dealing with the operation of elementary school libraries. Theme-based bibliographies, book reviews, and reviews of media are included. One author or illustrator is profiled each issue. This magazine is published bimonthly during the school year.

> Order from: Linworth Publishing Inc.
> 480 E. Wilson Bridge Road, Ste L
> Worthington, OH 43085-9918
> 614-436-7107

➢ *The Lion and The Unicorn: A Critical Journal of Children's Literature*

This semi-annual, peer-reviewed journal of children's literature and culture is usually published as themed issues but occasionally addresses a range of general topics. The journal contains content and literary analyses, essays and articles, professional book reviews, and announcements. Critical articles, essays, and reviews focus broadly across the full spectrum of issues in the scholarly field of children's literature, especially focusing on cultural, social, and political concerns. Occasionally, the pedagogical implications of literature within the broader sociocultural context are also addressed. The audience for this journal includes scholars working in the areas of literary and cultural studies as well as educators, librarians, and authors and illustrators of children's literature.

> Order from: Johns Hopkins University Press
> Journals Division
> 2715 North Charles Street
> Baltimore MD 21218-4319
> 410-516-6987
> 800-548-1784.

➢ *Multicultural Review*

This journal provides reviews of multicultural materials and information on the subject of multiculturalism. Articles and research are also published relating to various issues of multiculturalism. Reviews of books for children and young adults as well as audio-visual materials and software are included in this quarterly journal.

> Order from: *Multicultural Review*
> Greenwood Publishing Group, Inc.
> 88 Post Road West
> Box 5007
> Westport, CT 06881-5007
> 203-226-3571

➢ *The New Advocate*

Published four times a year, this peer-reviewed journal focuses on the connections between literature and teaching. Categories for articles are creative process, concepts and themes, and practical reflections. The articles include essays by authors and illustrators, practical reflections on the use of literature in the classroom, and research and theory on children's literature. Also included in each issue are reviews of new children's books and professional resources. The journal reaches out to a broad audience of classroom teachers, librarians, teacher educators, and authors and illustrators.

> Order from: *The New Advocate*
> 480 Washington Street
> Norwood, MA 02062
> 617-762-5577

➢ *The New York Times Book Review*

Reviews of children's books appear weekly in the column entitled "For Younger Readers." Twice a year (Fall and Spring) the "Book Reviews" section is devoted to reviewing children's books. In November and December, selected lists of outstanding children's books are published.

Order from: *The New York Times Book Review*
229 West 43rd Street
New York, New York 10036
800-631-2580

➢ *Primary Voices K–6*
This quarterly journal, published by the National Council of Teachers of English, is aimed at teachers and teacher educators. The current thinking of language arts educators is explored through short, practical articles. Each issue concentrates on a specific topic and includes a brief theoretical framework, classroom portraits, and reflections by the editors. A "literacy community" such as TAWL (Teachers Applying Whole Language) groups, writing projects, and school teams submits a proposal to NCTE and then develops, writes, and edits a specific issue of the journal. Bibliographies of professional books are also included.

Order from: National Council of Teachers of English
1111 W. Kenyon Road
Urbana, IL 61801-1096
217-328-3870
800-369-6283

➢ *The Reading Teacher*
This peer-reviewed journal of the International Reading Association is published eight times a year for an audience of teachers and teacher educators. It serves as a forum for current practice, theory, and research in the literacy education of children in elementary schools. Each issue contains reviews of current children's literature, and articles on the use of children's literature in the classroom are frequently included. The October issue features the winners of the "Children's Choices" award, an annual bibliography of books chosen by children as their favorite books. The

"Teachers' Choices" award winners appears in the November issue and include books that teachers rate as exceptional for curriculum use. The subscription cost is included in the membership fee.

Order from: International Reading Association
800 Barksdale Road
PO Box 8139
Newark, DE 19714-8139
302-731-1600
800-628-8508

➤ *School Library Journal*

This monthly journal reviews more than 85 percent of the new books for children and young adults published each year. Reviews are categorized by fiction or nonfiction at four age levels. Outstanding books receive a star rating and are included in the annual list of "Best Books" in the December issue. Children's books in Spanish are frequently reviewed, and reviews of audio-visual materials and software appear monthly. Each edition contains articles about children's literature, interviews with authors, and issues and research relating to library services for children in school or public library settings.

Order from: *School Library Journal*
PO Box 1978
Marion, OH 43306-2078
800-842-1669 (Continental United States)
614-382-3322 (Alaska, Hawaii, Canada, and all other countries)

➤ *Science and Children*

This peer-reviewed journal of the National Science Teachers Association is devoted to preschool through middle school science teaching. A column reviewing recent science books and audio-visual materials appears in each of the eight issues a year. A list of notable science books for the year appears each spring. Subscription cost is included in the membership fee.

Order from: National Science Teachers Association
1840 Wilson Blvd.
Arlington, VA 22201-3000
703-243-7100

➤ *Social Education*
Published seven times a year by the National Council for the Social Studies, this journal focuses on issues related to social studies. Articles and bibliographies often highlight children's books related to a theme. Book reviews appear monthly with the April/May issue featuring a list of the notable books in social studies for the year. Subscription cost is included in the membership fee.

Order from: National Council for the Social Studies
3501 Newark Street, N.W.
Washington, DC 20016-3199
202-966-7840

➤ *Teaching and Learning Literature*
Published five times a year, this journal provides teacher educators, teachers, and parents with a literary perspective on genres, books, authors, and the use of literature in classrooms and homes. Features include articles on literary principles and genres, interviews with adults involved in children's literature, and reviews of books for children and young adults.

Order from: *Teaching and Learning Literature*
Box 696
Middlebury, VT 05753

➤ *VOYA*
Voice of Youth Advocates (*VOYA*) is published bimonthly from April through February. Each issue contains articles

related to young adult literature, bibliographies, and reviews of books. A book review code is indicated at the beginning of the review section. Each book is coded according to quality, popularity, and grade level interest. The intended audience for this journal is those individuals working with or interested in young adult literature.

Order from: Scarecrow Press
Dept. VOYA
52 Liberty Street
PO Box 4167
Metuchen, NJ 08840
908-548-8600
800-537-7107

➤ *The WEB: Wonderfully Exciting Books*
A periodical issued three times a year by the Center for Language, Literature and Reading of The Ohio State University, each *WEB* contains reviews of books by teachers and librarians, reports of children's responses to these books, and a "web of possibilities" for integrating books into the school curriculum. Each issue features a genre, author, or theme.

Order from: *The WEB*
The Ohio State University
Room 200
Ramseyer Hall
Columbus, OH 43210

➤ *Wilson Library Bulletin*
This monthly bulletin contains discussions and reviews of adult and children's books. Reviews of library reference books, literary awards, biographical author sketches, and monthly displays are also included. The October issue is devoted to children's books. An annual best books list appears in December.

Order from: H.W. Wilson Company
950 University Avenue
Bronx, NY 10452-9978
800-367-6770

➤ *Young Children*

Published six times a year, this is a peer-reviewed journal of the National Association for the Education of Young Children. The journal intends to keep members of NAEYC abreast of the latest developments in early childhood education through research articles that focus on classroom practice. Articles on children's literature are included as well as reviews of children's and professional books and audio-visual materials.

Order from: NAEYC
1509 16th St., N.W.
Washington, DC 20036-1426
202-232-8777
800-424-2460

	Articles on literature in the classroom	Essays on children's literature	Research on children's literature	Author and illustrator features	Reviews of children's & adolescent literature	Reviews of professional resources	Reviews of audio-visual materials	Themed bibliographies	Annual best books list	Information on conference and book awards
Appraisal					*R					
Bookbird		X	X	X	X	X		X		X
Booklist		X			R	X	X	X		
Book Links	X	X		X	X			X	X	
The Book Report				X	X	X	X	X		
BCCB					R	X			X	
Canadian Children's Literature		X	X		X	X				X
CBC Features	X	X		X	X	X		X	X	
Childhood Education	X	X			X	X	X	X	X	X
Children's Literature		X	X			X				X
Children's Literature Association Quarterly		X	X		X	X				X
Children's Literature in Education		X	X							
Dragon Lode	X	X			X			X		X
English Journal										
The Five Owls		X			X			X		
Horn Book	X	X		X	X	X			X	X
Journal of Children's Literature	X	X	X	X	X	X		X	X	X
Journal of Reading	X		X	X	X	X			X	
Journal of Youth Services in Libraries		X	X	X	X	X		X	X	X
Kirkus					X					
Kliatt		X			X			X		
Language Arts	X		X	X	X	X		X	X	X
Library Talk	X	X		X	X	X	X	X		

	Articles on literature in the classroom	Essays on children's literature	Research on children's literature	Author and illustrator features	Reviews of children's & adolescent literature	Reviews of professional resources	Reviews of audio-visual materials	Themed bibliographies	Annual best books list	Information on conference and book awards
The Lion and the Unicorn		X	X			X				X
Multicultural Review		X	X		X	X	X	X		
The New Advocate	X	X	X	X	X	X		X		
The NY Times Book Review					X				X	
Primary Voices	X						X			
The Reading Teacher	X	X	X	X	X	X		X	X	X
School Library Journal		X	X	X	X	X	X	X	X	X
Science and Children	X				X	X	X		X	X
Social Education	X				X			X	X	
Teaching and Learning Literature	X	X		X	X	X				X
Voya		X			X	X		X		
The WEB	X			X	X	X		X		
Wilson Library Bulletin				X	X	X	X		X	X
Young Children	X				X	X	X			X

* Reviews contain a rating system

Other Journals Containing Research on Children's Literature

➤ *Elementary School Journal*
This refereed journal is issued five times a year and contains original research, reviews of research, and conceptual analyses for researchers and teachers who are interested in elementary education. Some issues have a specific theme and include an introduction to the topic. Reviews of professional books are also published.

> Order from: University of Chicago Press
> Journals Division
> PO Box 37005
> Chicago, IL 60637

➤ *Journal of Reading Behavior: A Journal of Literacy*
Published by the National Reading Conference, this journal is issued quarterly. It contains research articles, reviews, and analyses along with theoretical essays concerning reading, writing, and oral language. Professional book reviews and invited articles by recognized scholars in literacy are also included. Subscription is available as part of membership in the organization.

> Order from: The National Reading Conference
> 200 N. Michigan Avenue
> Chicago, IL 60601
> 312-541-1272

➤ *National Reading Conference Yearbook*
This refereed yearbook is published annually by the National Reading Conference and includes recent, original pieces of research presented at the Annual Meeting of the

National Reading Conference. This research covers a wide range of topics related to basic literacy processes, learning from text, emergent literacy, special populations, classroom instruction, teacher development, literacy and language diversity, policy issues, and assessment. Research on reader response and literature based classrooms is included in each yearbook. The primary audience for this yearbook is university and teacher researchers in reading and language education.

Order from: The National Reading Conference, Inc.
11 E. Hubbard, Suite 200
Chicago, IL 60611
312-329-2512

➤ *Reading Horizons*
This refereed quarterly journal, published by the College of Education at Western Michigan University, is devoted to articles on the teaching of reading at all levels. It contains both articles and research findings covering all aspects of reading, many of which center on the use of children's literature. Authors published in this journal must be subscribers.

Order from: Western Michigan University
Reading Horizons
Kalamazoo, MI 49008

➤ *Reading Improvement*
This quarterly journal publishes research and theoretical papers on the teaching of reading at all age levels. It is intended for those who want a better understanding of the reading process and wish to improve their teaching. The majority of articles are research on the reading process; however, there are also articles on other aspects of literacy, including writing.

Order from: Project Innovation of Mobile
Box 8508 Spring Hill Station
Mobile, AL 36679

➤ *Reading Research and Instruction*
This quarterly refereed journal publishes articles dealing with research and instruction in reading education and allied fields. Articles are concerned with instructional practices and pure research of special interest to reading and literacy educators. The journal is a publication of The College Reading Association.

> Order from: Dr. E. Sutton Flynt
> Publications Business Manager
> Dept. Curriculum and Instruction
> Pittsburg State University
> Pittsburg, KS 66762

➤ *Reading Research Quarterly*
This refereed research journal is published quarterly by the International Reading Association and contains extensive and detailed articles that focus on theory and research in reading. The journal generally publishes only four articles in each issue. The topics range from reading interest studies to research on instructional practices and critical reviews of research on a particular topic. The major audience for this journal is university and teacher researchers in reading education. A subscription includes membership in IRA.

> Order from: International Reading Association
> 800 Barksdale Road
> PO Box 8139
> Newark, DE 19714-8139
> 302-731-1600
> 800-628-8508

➤ *Research in the Teaching of English*
This refereed journal includes both original research and scholarly essays concerning language teaching and learning from preschool through adult levels. Published four times a year by the National Council of Teachers of English,

this journal is multidisciplinary in nature and seeks to provide the opportunity for open discussion of issues by educators in the fields of English and languages arts. A subscription includes membership in National Council of Teachers of English.

Order from: National Council of Teachers of English
111 W. Kenyon Road
Urbana, IL 61801-1096
217-328-3870
800-369-6283

➤ *Teacher Research: The Journal of Classroom Inquiry*
This peer-reviewed journal is focused on balancing research reports with explanations of classroom inquiry. It publishes teachers' reports of research findings from their own classrooms as well as honest and personal accounts of teachers in the midst of completing research studies and solving problems of time and technique. The articles are written by both experienced and novice teacher researchers in a teacher-to-teacher voice. Each publication has a theme such as "Communities." There are two publications a year.

Order from: Teacher Research Journal
Johnson Press
49 Sheridan Avenue
Albany, NY 12210

Centers Conducting Research on Children's Literature

Reports on research can be obtained by writing to the following centers:

Center for the Study of Books in Spanish for Children and Adolescents
California State
University, San Marcos
San Marcos, CA
92096-0001
619-752-4070

National Research Center on Literature Teaching & Learning
State University of
New York
1400 Washington Avenue
Albany, NY 12222
518-442-5026

National Reading Research Center
318 Aderhold Hall
University of Georgia
Athens, GA 30602-7125
706-542-3674

2101 J.M. Patterson
Building
University of Maryland
College Park, MD 20742
301-405-8035

International Institute for Children's Literature and Research
Mayerhofgasse 6
A-1040
Vienna, Austria
1-5-52834

International Research Society for Children's Literature
Route de Matasset
F-33140
Cadaujac, France

International Youth Library
Schloss Blutenburg
81247
Munich, Germany
89-8112028

Journals Searched by Hand for Research Bibliography

Australian Journal of Language and Literacy

Canadian Children's Literature

Canadian Journal of English Language Arts (formerly *Highway One*)

Childhood Education

Children's Literature (Annuals of The Modern Language Association)

Children's Literature in Education

Children's Literature Association Quarterly

Curriculum Inquiry

Educational Research Quarterly

Elementary School Journal

English Education

English in Australia

English Journal

English Quarterly

Journal for the National Association for Bilingual Education

Journal of Educational Research

Journal of Reading

Journal of Reading Behavior

Journal of Reading Education

Journal of Research in Reading

Journal of Teacher Research

Journal of Youth Services in Libraries (formerly *Top of the News*)

Language Arts

Learning Disability Quarterly

Library and Information Science Research

Library Trends

The Lion and the Unicorn

The New Advocate

Primary Voices

Reading

Reading Horizons

Reading Improvement

Reading Research and Instruction

Reading Research Quarterly

Reading Teacher

Research in the Teaching of English

Reflections on Canadian Literacy (formerly *Reading-Canada-Lecture*)

School Library Journal

School Library Media Quarterly

Social Science Quarterly

Theory into Practice

Yearbook of the National Reading Conference

Young Children

Section III: Professional Books on Children's Literature

The tremendous interest in children's literature and its role in the curriculum is reflected not only in the research reported in this book but also in the large number of professional books on children's literature currently available to educators. Educators have turned to professional resources for theoretical and practical support as they have moved away from basal readers and text-driven curriculum toward real books and learning environments where readers actively and critically construct meaning. The professional books in this section support educators in considering the literary and learning theories behind this paradigm shift and the struggles of other educators who have reconceptualized their own teaching philosophies and understandings about literature and learning. The books range from theoretical discussions of children's literature and the transactional process to descriptions of literature-based classrooms, lists of activities with children's books, and extensive annotated bibliographies of books on particular topics.

The majority of books in this section were written by either university professors of education and literary criticism or classroom teachers. There has been a notable increase in the number of books by teachers and teacher researchers, and their work has had a significant effect on curriculum reform.

While a large percentage of the books cited describe the use of children's literature in the elementary school, there are a growing number of books on using literature in the middle school and high school. A few books focus on preschool and early literacy experiences. In contrast to the books on curriculum, most of the theoretical books are written by university faculty from the fields of literary criticism and English education who base their work on responses of students ages 12 or older.

The changes in curriculum and instructional strategies evident in some of these professional books reflect the grass roots movement toward a philosophy of purposeful natural learning and whole language. The reader response theories of Louise Rosenblatt are referenced throughout the work of teacher researchers, as are the works of theorists explicating Rosenblatt. Most of the books contain lengthy bibliographies of children's literature or professional books, so they provide access to many other references that can support educators in their explorations.

Not yet visible in published volumes are books describing inquiry-based learning using children's literature, especially nonfiction. Most educators are still focused on literature-based curriculum and reading or language arts instruction instead of looking more broadly at inquiry as the base of curriculum and schooling and the ways that literature can support inquiry.

There are professional books on children's literature and curriculum that we chose not to include in this section. These books were ones that "basalized" the use of children's literature and primarily consisted of lists of vocabulary words, comprehension questions, and activities. We also did not include reading and language arts methods textbooks. The books we did include reflect a wide range of theoretical beliefs about literature and learning. Many of the books included in the category of Collections of Activities, for example, are based in a direct teaching model in which teachers develop and deliver curriculum to children instead of a collaborative model of teachers and students negotiating and planning curriculum together. Some books are strongly based in transactional theories of reading and literary response while others come from interactional theories of readers and texts.

The sheer volume of current professional books on children's literature necessitated dividing them into categories. Although many of the books could have been placed into more than one category, a book was categorized according to its major focus (for example, genre or reading instruction) and its organizational format (such as bibliographic lists or chapters describing classroom practices). Books on poetry, for example, can be found in the sections on annotated bibliographies, author studies, collections, language arts curriculum, genres, and literature discussion.

Theoretical Foundations of Literature in the Classroom

This group contains major pieces of literary theory and analysis and commentary on those theories. Rosenblatt, Britton, Holdaway, and Langer are among the theorists included. Their work provides the foundation for much of the research and practice in children's literature.

Beach, R. (1993). *A teacher's introduction to reader response theories*. Urbana, IL: National Council of Teachers of English.

> This comprehensive overview of reader-response theories describes the relationship between reader and text from textual, experiential, social, psychological, and cultural theoretical perspectives. Acknowledging that theory shapes practice, the relationships between reader, text, and context are described so that teachers may examine the assumptions driving their own teaching and consider their goals in teaching literature.

Britton, J. (1993). *Literature in its place*. Portsmouth, NH: Heinemann.

> Called a "gift" to English teachers throughout the world, this book is the embodiment of Britton's long career in literary theory. He places literature at the center of human experience and relates that experience to literary interactions. Chapters include the role of inner speech, make-believe, the values of poetry, and the role of imagination in the literary experience.

Clifford, J. (Ed.). (1991). *The experience of reading: Louise Rosenblatt and reader-response theory*. Portsmouth, NH: Heinemann.

> Authored by reading and literary theorists, this book focuses on Rosenblatt's reader-response theory (see p. 196). The essays demonstrate to teachers of high school

and college English that Rosenblatt's emphasis on the centrality of the reader makes her a teacher's theorist, as do her insights into the social nature of learning and the democratic possibilities of reading.

Holdaway, D. (1979). *The foundations of literacy*. Sydney, Australia: Ashton Scholastic.

This important work has led the way to educational change in the field of early literacy. Holdaway explores learning to read from a developmental learning perspective based on his years of research and classroom development. This book is a valuable resource for educators who want to support children in their efforts to become proficient readers and writers.

Karolides, N.J. (Ed.). (1992). *Reader response in the classroom: Evoking and interpreting meaning in literature*. New York: Longman.

The chapters in this book explain and interpret the reader response theory of Louise Rosenblatt. Many of the essays bridge the gap to practice by demonstrating strategies for implementing reader response theories in the classroom. Several specific literary works are highlighted and actual classroom transcripts are included.

Langer, J.A. (Ed.). (1992). *Literature instruction: A focus on student response*. Urbana, IL: National Council of Teachers of English.

Written by major researchers in literature instruction, these chapters call for a shift in focus away from the teacher and text toward student response. The authors argue that the long-held belief in a single interpretation of text leads to ineffective teaching and learning.

Moran, C., & Penfield, E.F. (1990). *Conversations: Contemporary critical theory and the teaching of literature*. Urbana, IL: National Council of Teachers of English.

Developed from two summer institutes sponsored by NCTE, this book reflects recent conversations about literary theory and teaching literature in the classroom.

Topics include contemporary critical theory, teachers'
voices, and theory as it relates to classroom practice.

Probst, R.E. (1988). *Response and analysis: Teaching literature in junior and senior high school*. Portsmouth, NH:
Heinemann.

Drawing heavily on the theories of Rosenblatt, Probst
argues that literary meaning resides within the transaction between the reader and the text and is created within the individual reader. This book demonstrates how
teachers can lead students to analyze both a text and
their reading of it through response. A comprehensive
bibliography of adolescent literature is included.

Rosenblatt, L. (1978). *The reader, the text, the poem*. Carbondale, IL: Southern Illinois University Press.

This straightforward analysis of the role of the reader in
reconceptualizing a literary work provides answers to
controversial questions of literary theory. Rosenblatt's
concepts of transactional reading and efferent and aesthetic stance are clearly presented. The book is written
for the general public as well as the literary specialist.

Rosenblatt, L. (1983). *Literature as exploration* (4th ed.).
New York: The Modern Language Association of America.

First published in 1938, this is the fourth revised edition
of an influential book on the personal experience of literature and the interaction of text and reader. Rosenblatt's transactional theories of literary interpretation
are explained, and the social concepts that influence the
study of literature are described. Rosenblatt further discusses the background and experiences of the reader as
the source of literary sensitivity and insight.

Literature Discussion and Response

The books in this group describe instructional strategies and curriculum based on reader response theory. Topics range from talking about books to response journals to art to drama.

Cullinan, B.E. (Ed.). (1993). *Children's voices: Talk in the classroom*. Newark, DE: International Reading Association.

> Cullinan has brought together chapters written by experts in their respective fields of classroom talk, including Sam Sebesta, Kathy Short, and Julie Wollman-Bonilla. The authors explore storytelling, drama, choral reading, literature discussions, and literature circles.

Holland, K.E., Hungerford, R.A., & Ernst, S.B. (Eds.). (1993). *Journeying: Children responding to literature*. Portsmouth, NH: Heinemann.

> This book is a collection of university and teacher explorations and research based on Louise Rosenblatt's transactional theory of reader response. The chapters cut across age levels to yield insights into how children create meaning from stories, how literacy skills are enhanced, and the role of teachers in facilitating their response. Topics addressed include response to different genres, processes of response, developmental characteristics, cultural responses, and teachers' influences. The contributors also share ideas about successful classroom practices.

Nelms, B.F. (Ed.). (1989). *Literature in the classroom: Readers, texts, and contexts*. Urbana, IL: National Council of Teachers of English.

> Discussed here are responses to literature in various contexts as experienced by 1st graders, 7th graders, high school students, college teachers, researchers, and theo-

rists. An introductory chapter argues for the importance of reader response theory, and the rest of the book contains research studies and reflective pieces concerning student responses to literature, interpretive approaches to text, and social dimensions of literature. Theory and practice are integrated to support response-based teaching.

Newkirk, T., with McClure, P. (1992). *Listening in: Children talk about books (and other things)*. Portsmouth, NH: Heinemann.

Filled with transcripts of children's dialogue, this book invites teachers to explore the endless possibilities of children's talk about literature, even when that talk appears to be "off topic." The text-dominated, question-controlled pedagogy that prevails in U.S. classrooms is challenged as the authors explore the oral culture of children and the learning opportunities this culture provides in a 2nd grade classroom.

Parsons, L. (1990). *Response journals*. Portsmouth, NH: Heinemann.

This short, practical guide to the use of response journals gives a step-by-step system for implementing these journals in the classroom. The author discusses the use of response journals for responding to media and literature, evaluation of journals, development of small group discussion, and student-teacher conferences.

Peterson, R., & Eeds, M. (1990). *Grand conversations: Literature groups in action*. Ontario, Canada: Scholastic.

The authors point out that literature is its own content area and that it has value in and of itself, not just in its use to teach reading or other content areas. The major emphasis is on the importance of dialogue in responding to literature in a literature program that has four basic components: home and story, read-aloud, extensive reading, and intensive reading. The authors discuss teaching about story through literary elements such as mood and character. Various forms for assessment are included.

Pierce, K.M., & Gilles, C.J. (Eds.). (1993). *Cycles of meaning: Exploring the potential of talk in learning communities*. Portsmouth, NH: Heinemann.

> The chapters in this edited book grew out of the explorations of a teacher study group and the work of teacher and university researchers focused on talk in the classroom. The chapters draw heavily on the writings of Douglas Barnes, a contributor and consultant. Clear examples are provided for the creation of collaborative communities, involvement in literature discussion groups, and the creation of concepts through talk. Many specific examples, transcripts of discussions, and teacher reflections are included.

Purves, A.C., Rogers, T., & Soter, A.O. (1990). *How porcupines make love II: Teaching a response-centered literature curriculum*. White Plains, NY: Longman.

> The authors' goal is to make middle school and high school teachers aware of reader-response theory and its implications for literature instruction and curriculum. The authors demonstrate how a response-centered curriculum brings students to a greater understanding of all forms of literature.

Short, K.G., & Pierce, K.M. (Eds.). (1990). *Talking about books: Creating literate communities*. Portsmouth, NH: Heinemann.

> The chapters in this book are written by classroom teachers and teacher educators on the value and use of literature discussions in classrooms. The work is divided into three major sections: establishing a context for literate communities, organizing the classroom to support talk about literature, and making decisions about curriculum and learning. Each chapter is followed by bibliographies of children's and professional books.

Sloan, G.D. (1984). *The child as critic: Teaching literature in elementary and middle schools* (2nd ed.). New York: Teachers College Press.

Sloan builds a case for a program of literature study and composition grounded in the archetypal literary theories of Northrop Frye. The first section explores literary theories and research and the child's development of literary understandings. Later sections present a comprehensive program that invites teachers to make literature central to their classrooms. Strategies for teaching literary criticism and chapters on composing are included.

Wollman-Bonilla, J. (1991). *Response journals: Inviting students to think and write about literature.* New York: Scholastic.

This book is a practical, easy-to-use guide for teachers who are getting started with response journals. It will help teachers build community as children explore and interpret literature for themselves.

Surveys of Children's Literature

This is a short collection of textbooks used in children's literature courses on many university campuses with preservice and inservice teachers. They provide a broad survey of genres and the most popular literature available for classroom use. These texts come from education, library science, and English literature perspectives and are updated every few years to include the most recent publications. Because these books survey the field of children's literature, teachers often continue to use them as references for locating information on authors, illustrators, genres, and titles.

Cullinan, B.E., & Galda, L. (1994). *Literature and the Child* (3rd ed.). Fort Worth, TX: Harcourt Brace.

> This edition of a comprehensive textbook has been shortened and changed significantly from earlier editions. The three sections of the text address the broader context of children's literature and response, the genres, and issues related to multiculturalism and curriculum. The text is filled with author and illustrator profiles and teaching ideas. It begins with the reading theory of Louise Rosenblatt and concludes with planning for a literature curriculum.

Huck, C.S., Hepler, S., & Hickman, J. (1992). *Children's literature in the elementary school* (5th ed.). New York: Holt, Rinehart and Winston.

> This comprehensive and detailed text covers all aspects of children's literature and includes three broad categories: books and children, knowing children's literature, and developing literature program. Also included are extensive bibliographies, genre and thematic groupings, and tips for evaluating literature.

Lynch-Brown, C., & Tomlinson, C. (1993). *Essentials of children's literature*. Boston, MA: Allyn & Bacon.

> This concise text was written for the undergraduate audience in beginning survey courses. The text primarily focuses on specific genres and categories of literature but also includes short sections on the values of children's literature and curriculum and teaching strategies. Well-known books are given as examples, but lengthy book reviews and bibliographies are not included.

Nodelman, P. (1992). *The pleasures of children's literature*. New York: Longman.

> Nodelman's goal in writing this introduction to children's literature was to make use of recent research from as many different disciplines as possible. Nodelman also uses his own work in literary studies to provide adults with contexts and strategies of comprehension for understanding and enjoying children's literature and to suggest ways that children can be taught these strategies and contexts.

Norton, D.E. (1991). *Through the eyes of a child* (3rd ed.). New York: Macmillan.

> Chapters in this comprehensive children's literature text include history, evaluation, artists and illustrations, multicultural literature, and the various genres. Boxed articles deal with current topics such as censorship, social issues, racism, and historical bias. The text overflows with bibliographies.

Russell, D.L. (1994). *Literature for children: A short introduction* (2nd ed.). Longman: New York.

> Organized by genre, this general text is a concise yet accessible supplement to the actual reading of children's literature. Designed for pre-service and in-service teachers, the text provides a general overview of picture books, folk literature, poetry, fantasy, realism and nonfiction. The book focuses on discussions of genre, history, and current issues and trends but does not include extensive bibliographies of books.

Sebesta, S., & Donelson, K. (Eds.). (1993). *Inspiring litera-cy: Literature for children and young adults*. New Brunswick, NJ: Transaction Publishers.

> This book, which first appeared in *Publishing Research Quarterly* (Fall 1991 and Spring 1992), examines what children read and what makes them want to read. Chapters explore trends in publishing, revolutionary changes in how literature is taught, and the status of multicultural literature. Contributors include Robert Probst, Bernice Cullinan, and Barbara Keifer.

Stewig, J.W. (1988). *Children and literature* (2nd ed.). Boston, MA: Houghton Mifflin.

> This thorough study of children's literature includes numerous techniques teachers can use to evoke response. The text is arranged by genre, and tips for evaluating each genre are included. Suggestions for further study, related reading for adults, and extensive bibliographies follow each chapter.

Sutherland, Z., & Arbuthnot, M.H. (1991). *Children and books*. New York: HarperCollins.

> This overview of the field of children's literature highlights children's authors and illustrators in each genre. Included are frequent "Viewpoint" quotes in which the authors reflect on their genre and their work. Chapters focus on genre and age levels as well as evaluation, illustration, informational books, and books across the curriculum. Extensive annotated bibliographies are found throughout.

Sociopolitical and Cultural Issues in Children's Literature

The majority of these professional books focus on multicultural issues in children's literature, especially in relation to the ways in which people of color are depicted. Other books address social or political issues in children's literature.

Bacon, B. (Ed.). (1988). *How much truth do we tell children? The politics of children's literature.* Minneapolis, MN: Marxist Educational Press.

> Part of the book series "Marxist Dimensions," these essays explore children's literature against the backdrop of current social, political, economic, and moral values that shape the world. Topics include the Holocaust, fairy tales, racist stereotypes, biography, and historical perspectives.

Dyson, A.H., & Genishi, C. (Eds.). (1994). *The need for story: Cultural diversity in classroom and community.* Urbana, IL: National Council of Teachers of English.

> Contributors to this volume explore the nature of story, its connection to the diverse landscape of our society, and its power in the classroom. The book emphasizes the complex relationships among story, ethnicity, and gender and addresses issues related to both oral and written stories. The authors address concerns about how to most effectively serve increasingly diverse student populations, and they offer vivid examples of the need for and the power of story.

Harris, V.J. (Ed.). (1992). *Teaching multicultural literature in grades K–8.* Norwood, MA: Christopher Gordon.

> Harris gathered experts in the field of children's literature from a variety of cultures and asked them to write chapters about using literature from their culture in the

classroom. The resulting book describes ways of using literature from African American, Mexican American, Asian Pacific American, Native American, and other cultures. Small and large presses are referenced with phone numbers.

Lurie, A. (1990). *Don't tell the grown-ups: Subversive children's literature*. Boston, MA: Little, Brown.

Pulitzer Prize–winning novelist Alison Lurie explores the theme that the best-loved children's books tend to challenge rather than uphold respectable adult values. She examines books such as *Alice's Adventures in Wonderland, Peter Pan, Winnie-the-Pooh,* and *The Tale of Peter Rabbit.* Lurie points out that enduring children's books do not improve children morally; rather they empathize with the child and value the imaginative and unrestrained agenda of childhood.

MacCann, D., & Woodard, G. (1985). *The Black American in books for children: Readings in racism* (2nd ed.). Metuchen, NJ: Scarecrow Press.

This work is a collection of individually authored chapters, first published elsewhere, that deal with the sensitive issue of racism in children's literature. The authors are discouraged by the lack of an accurate portrayal of black culture through text and illustrations. Among the notable contributors are Rudine Sims Bishop, Walter Dean Myers, Dorothy Sterling, and Eloise Greenfield.

Sims, R. (1982). *Shadow and substance: Afro-American experience in contemporary children's fiction*. Urbana, IL: National Council of Teachers of English.

The purpose of this monograph is to enable teachers and librarians to make socially responsible choices when selecting children's literature about African Americans. Critical of the ways the African American experience is distorted, Sims includes extensive bibliographies of recommended titles.

Slapin, B., & Seale, D. (Eds.). (1992). *Through Indian eyes: The native experience in books for children*. Philadelphia, PA: New Society.

> This collection of essays by Native Americans deals with the impact of stereotyping on children. Included are over 100 short reviews critiquing children's books on Native Americans and many examples of original poetry, art, and stories by Native Americans. Extensive bibliographies and indexes make this work easy to use.

West, M.I. (1988). *Trust your children: Voices against censorship in children's literature*. New York: Neal-Schuman.

> Each chapter in this book contains an interview with an author of a book frequently targeted by censors, publishers, or members of anti-censorship organizations such as People for the American Way. The interviews probe why certain books may come under attack and how the authors and publishers have responded to censorship attempts. Authors include Judy Blume, Norma Klein, Maurice Sendak, John Steptoe, and Roald Dahl.

Genre Studies in the Classroom

This group of books is subdivided by specific genres such as poetry or nonfiction. The major focus of these books is the genre itself, either on understanding that genre at a theoretical level or on ways to develop classroom studies of that genre. Many other books on particular genres can be found in other categories.

Folk and Fairy Tales

Blatt, G.T. (Ed). (1993). *Once upon a folktale: Capturing the folklore process with children*. New York: Teachers College Press.

> These chapters are written by distinguished authorities in children's literature who share their experiences using folklore in the classroom, home, and community. The book is divided into three major sections: bringing children and folklore together, understanding the folklore process, and making connections to other forms of literature.

Bosma, B. (1992). *Fairy tales, fables, legends, and myths: Using folk literature in your classroom* (2nd ed.). New York: Teachers College Press.

> This practical handbook is designed to guide teachers in the use of folk literature in the classroom. This second edition contains a chapter on multicultural folktales along with strategies for enhancing comprehension, critical reading, writing, and the arts. A special section focuses on folk literature in the upper grades. The last chapter contains an annotated bibliography of over 180 pieces of folk literature.

Picture books

Benedict, S., & Carlisle, L. (Eds.). (1992). *Beyond words: Picture books for older readers and writers.* Portsmouth, NH: Heinemann.

> The chapters in this book deal with the uses of picture books with all ages. Several children's authors share their insights along with educators who discuss their use of picture books to encourage creative processes and critical thinking. A bibliography of picture books is also included.

Marantz, S.S. (1992). *Picture books for looking and learning: Awakening visual perceptions through the art of children's books.* Phoenix, AZ: Oryx Press.

> The first two chapters provide the reader with a definition of a picture book and its parts and an introduction to the various media used in picture books. The text analyzes the illustrations in a wide variety of well-known picture books. Questions and queries to share with children are also provided.

Schwarcz, J.H., & Schwarcz, C. (1991). *The picture book comes of age: Looking at childhood through the art of illustration.* Chicago, IL: American Library Association.

> These essays examine the picture book as a potentially powerful medium that relates to children's experiences and supports the development of humanistic responsibilities. The book is intended to help the adult reader explore and evaluate picture books in the context of the child's development. Chapters explore stress, love, grandparents, emergence of identity, a sense of place, and social action for the disadvantaged.

Poetry

Denman, G.A. (1988). *When you've made it your own: Teaching poetry to young people.* Portsmouth, NH: Heinemann.

Introduced by Bill Martin Jr. as "Johnny Poemseeder," the author offers a practical and useable guide for teaching poetry. He addresses many of the problems teachers have encountered in the past and "demystifies" the teaching of poetry across the curriculum. Extensive resource lists are designed to bring focus to the study of poetry.

Graves, D. (1992). *Explore poetry: The reading/writing teacher's companion.* Portsmouth, NH: Heinemann.

One of a series of five volumes primarily focused on writing, this book introduces poetry to teachers through their own experiences writing in the genre. The first section of the book addresses the reading of poetry with children. "Actions," scattered throughout the work, are designed to promote discovery within the classroom.

Heard, G. (1989). *For the good of the earth and sun: Teaching poetry.* Portsmouth, NH: Heinemann.

Heard, a well-known poet and writing consultant, has crafted this book for teachers of poetry. Designed to accommodate students of all ages, the book begins with the reading of poetry, then explores topics such as conferring, white space, language, and form. An annotated bibliography of poetry for children is included.

Hopkins, L.B. (1987). *Pass the poetry please.* New York: HarperCollins.

This new, updated version of a book first published in 1972 overflows with ideas for bringing poetry into the lives of children. Twenty brief biographies of contemporary poets are included along with bibliographies of their poetry books.

Larrick, N. (1991). *Let's do a poem: Introducing poetry to children through listening, singing, chanting, impromptu, choral reading, body movement, dance, and dramatization.* New York: Delacorte.

This handbook is filled with ideas for bringing poetry and children together in lively, innovative ways. Designed for preschool through junior high, the work includes extensive sections about using poetry with music, choral reading, and movement. Annotated bibliographies of poetry books are included.

McClure, A., Harrison, P., & Reed, S. (1990). *Sunrises and songs: Reading and writing poetry in the elementary classroom*. Portsmouth, NH: Heinemann.

> The authors cover every aspect of a complete poetry program for the classroom based on their experiences as teachers and researchers. Reading, writing, sharing, presenting, and discussion techniques are included. An annotated bibliography of poetry closes the volume.

Taxel, J. (Ed.). (1993). Fanfare. *The Christopher Gordon Children's Literature Annual, 1,* 1–143.

> This premiere edition, offered by Christopher Gordon, focuses on poetry for children and is available to all subscribers of *The New Advocate*. The collection is introduced by Myra Cohen Livingston's piece "Poetry and Self" and the companion piece "Poetry Outside My Skin" by Eve Merriam. Among the other contributors are Jane Yolen, Lee Galda, and Charles Temple.

Wolf, A. (1990). *Something is going to happen: Poetry performance in the classroom*. Asheville, NC: Iambic.

> This guide to poetry performance in the classroom was written to help teachers put on a poetry show and to augment classroom activities and learning. The early chapters discuss the basics of poetry performance. Later chapters include 15 poems, scripted and unscripted, and suggestions for performing them.

Informational Books

Freeman, E.B., & Person, D.G. (Eds.). (1992). *Using nonfiction trade books in the elementary classroom: From ants to zeppelins*. Urbana, IL: National Council of Teachers of English.

> The contributors, representing classroom teachers, college educators, librarians, and children's authors, discuss the genre of nonfiction, the link between nonfiction

and the elementary curriculum, and the use of nonfiction in the classroom. The collection includes numerous suggestions for classroom practice and an extensive bibliography of informational books.

Literature in the Reading and Language Arts Curriculum

The majority of these books are authored by classroom teachers and describe the use of children's literature in reading and integrated language arts curricula. These authors bring theory into practice and describe ways to expand the use of literature, especially in relation to reading and writing instruction. Included in this section are a number of books that have had a major impact on current educational thought.

Applebee, A.N. (1993). *Literature in the secondary school: Studies of curriculum and instruction in the United States.* Urbana, IL: National Council of Teachers of English.

> This book reports on four major studies of current practices in the teaching of literature in middle schools and secondary schools. Findings conclude that literary curriculum is neither as good as hoped nor as poor as critics claim. Applebee calls for a thorough reexamination of literature curriculum to provide teachers with a more unified framework that will better inform their practice.

Asselin, M., Pelland, N., & Shapiro, J. (1991). *Storyworlds: Linking minds and imagination through literature.* Ontario, Canada: Pippin.

> This book emphasizes the importance of the story experience for young children and explains how storyworld experiences can be expanded to other curriculum areas. Thematic approaches are discussed and two detailed themes, changes and space, are included with complete bibliographies.

Atwell, N. (1987). *In the middle: Writing, reading, and learning with adolescents.* Portsmouth, NH: Heinemann.

This personal account of how one teacher researcher integrated reading and writing workshops into her classroom addresses dialogue journals, book lists, student-to-student response, literary talk, and assessment. The book is written for middle school teachers but is easily adaptable to high school or upper elementary school.

Atwell, N. (Ed.). (1989). *Workshop 1 by and for teachers: Writing and literature.* Portsmouth, NH: Heinemann.

This annual, written by and for K–8 teachers, contains chapters on how students learn language and what teachers can do to help. The authors examine what is possible when teachers who understand real reading and writing bring them together so that students may engage in and enjoy both.

Atwell, N. (Ed.). (1990). *Workshop 2 by and for teachers: Beyond the Basal.* Portsmouth, NH: Heinemann.

This annual, written by and for K–8 teachers, is directed to teachers who want to implement a literature curriculum and have questions about organizing a classroom that is not dependent on the structure of a basal program.

Barton, B. (1986). *Tell me another: Storytelling and reading aloud at home, at school and in the community.* Portsmouth, NH: Heinemann.

In this practical book, Barton shares how to select and learn a story for storytelling, how to read stories to children, and how to use storytelling in the classroom. Many examples of stories and rhymes are included along with specific strategies for storytelling.

Bromley, K.D. (1991). *Webbing with literature: Creating story maps with children's books.* Boston, MA: Allyn and Bacon.

Webbing is a powerful tool that connects children with literature and the literary experience. Bromley presents a handbook for K–8 teachers that explores semantic webbing and story elements. The text includes an extensive annotated bibliography and over 125 actual webs of children's books.

Brown, H., & Cambourne, B. (1990). *Read and retell.* Portsmouth, NH: Heinemann.

> The authors describe, in detail, a retelling strategy teachers can use to help students explore a variety of genres and assess their control of language structures, text, and comprehension. Included are many reproducible stories to be read by children and instructions for retellings.

Carletti, S., Girard, S., & Willing, K. (1991). *The library/ classroom connection.* Portsmouth, NH: Heinemann.

> The movement toward whole language provides new potentials for collaborative relationships between teachers and librarians. This book presents strategies for promoting information literacy skills through teachers and librarians who plan curriculum together for both the classroom and library.

Cullinan, B.E. (Ed.). (1987). *Children's literature in the reading program.* Newark, DE: International Reading Association.

> This collection of chapters by experts in the field of children's literature is designed to guide teachers as they introduce and use literature in primary to 8th grade classrooms. The book contains the rationale for using literature, teaching strategies, and ideas for teaching higher order reading skills with literature.

Cullinan, B.E. (Ed.). (1992). *Invitation to read: More children's literature in the reading program.* Newark, DE: International Reading Association.

> This companion volume to *Children's Literature in the Reading Program* is again filled with teaching ideas for classroom use. Genre studies and thematic units form a large portion of the book. Censorship issues, tips for at-risk readers, and resources for locating children's literature are included. Hundreds of book titles are cited.

Feeley, J.T., Strickland, D.S., & Wepner, S.B. (Eds.). (1991). *Process reading and writing: A literature-based approach.* New York: Teachers College Press.

Designed to assist teachers in making the transition to a process-driven approach to language arts, this book is arranged in five sections. The first three sections address primary, middle elementary, and middle school, while the last two sections discuss special populations and change at the district level. Each chapter is written by a teacher or teacher educator on the cutting edge of change in U.S. schools.

Hagerty, P. (1992). *Reader's workshop: Real reading.* Ontario, Canada: Scholastic Canada.

This practical guide to why and how to use a reader's workshop includes minilessons, response, conferring, and sharing. A final section discusses getting started.

Hancock, J., & Hill, S. (Eds.). (1988). *Literature-based reading programs at work.* Portsmouth, NH: Heinemann.

First published in Australia, these chapters written by teachers address the whys and how-tos of changing to a literature reading program. Frequently asked questions are answered, and six different types of literature programs are highlighted.

Hart-Hewins, L., & Wells, J. (1990). *Real books for reading: Learning to read with children's literature.* Portsmouth, NH: Heinemann.

The authors invite teachers and parents to use real books for reading with children ages 3–8. Chapters cover evaluation of books, reading development, sharing books, classroom organization and components of a reading and writing program. An extensive bibliography of books for young children is included.

Hart-Hewins, L., & Wells, J. (1992). *Read it in the classroom: Organizing an interactive language arts program grades 4–9.* Portsmouth, NH: Heinemann.

This valuable resource was designed to guide grade 4–9 teachers in the use of literature in the classroom. Themed units and strategies cover a wide range of fiction, non-fiction, trade, and educational books. Extensive bibliographies are included.

Harwayne, S. (1992). *Lasting impressions: Weaving literature into the writing workshop*. Portsmouth, NH: Heinemann.

Harwayne offers readers an invitation to explore the diverse roles literature plays in the writing workshop. The book follows one class over an entire school year as children become passionate about literature and literary technique. Filled with teaching ideas and examples of student work, the book concludes with a bibliography of professional and children's books.

Hickman, J., & Cullinan, B.E. (Eds.). (1989). *Children's literature in the classroom: Weaving Charlotte's Web*. Norwood, MA: Christopher-Gordon.

This comprehensive book is written by authors well known for their work in the field of children's literature. The book is divided into three main sections: understanding the uses of literature, celebrating books and authors, and developing a literature program. Smaller sections on poetry, historical fiction, picture books, and fantasy are included along with extensive references.

Hickman, J., Cullinan, B.E., & Hepler, S. (Eds.). (1994). *Children's literature in the classroom: Extending Charlotte's Web*. Norwood, MA: Christopher-Gordon.

Concern over basalization of literature prompted Hickman, Cullinan, and Hepler to gather chapters written by teachers who know appropriate and stimulating ways to use literature in the classroom. Oral and written response, poetry, writing, fantasy, and illustrations are all presented in ways teachers can easily adapt to their classrooms. Other issues addressed in the text include planning for literature, creating a literate community, reading recovery, and early literacy.

Hill, S. (1986). *Books alive!: Using literature in the class-room*. Portsmouth, NH: Heinemann.

> Organized around four major themes, this book is filled with practical teaching ideas that bring children and books together. Themes include responding, featuring authors, focusing on story, and experiencing "great books." A bibliography of award-winning books in America, Great Britain, and Australia is included.

Hornsby, D., & Sukarna, D., with Parry, J. (1986). *Read on: A conference approach to reading*. Portsmouth, NH: Heinemann.

> This practical guide deals with organization, planning, response, record keeping, and evaluation of a reading program. Reproducibles are included.

Karelitz, E.B. (1993). *The author's chair and beyond: Language and literacy in the primary classroom*. Portsmouth, NH: Heinemann.

> While mainly a book about writing in the primary classroom, this volume has two important chapters on reading and children's literature. The reading community, whole class discussion, and reading conferences are among the topics included.

Kaywell, J. (Ed.). (1993). *Adolescent literature: As a complement to the classics*. Norwood, MA: Christopher-Gordon.

> These chapters, authored by teachers, discuss the use of a variety of literary classics in their reading program. Titles include *Anne Frank, Romeo and Juliet, Huckleberry Finn* and many others. Many references are included.

McConaghy, J. (1990). *Children learning through literature*. Portsmouth, NH: Heinemann.

> McConaghy, a teacher researcher, describes her own classroom practice of teaching reading and writing through children's literature. She shares her journey of becoming a lifelong learner along with her students by providing examples from her own reflections, student

writing samples, and suggestions about ways for others to incorporate literature into their own classrooms.

McTeague, F. (1992). *Shared reading in the middle and high school years*. Portsmouth, NH: Heinemann.

A practical guide for teachers helping children explore literature, this book includes ways of responding, collaborative approaches, themed units, poetry, storytelling, and suggestions for working with reluctant older readers.

Monseau, V.R., & Salvner, G.M. (1992). *Reading their world: The young adult novel in the classroom*. Portsmouth, NH: Boynton/Cook.

Written by educators and authors of adolescent literature, this book is designed to bring the young adult novel into its proper place in the English curriculum. Sections include reading, writing, and teaching the young adult novel. Special chapters are devoted to the issues of gender, cultural diversity, and censorship.

Reif, L. (1992). *Seeking diversity: Language arts with adolescents*. Portsmouth, NH: Heinemann.

Reif has taken the philosophies of Atwell, Romano, Murray, the Goodmans, Graves, and Calkins and made them her own by adapting them to her classroom. The book follows her students during September through June as they reveal themselves through their reading and writing. Many helpful forms, lists of best loved books, and descriptions of portfolios are included.

Robb, L. (1994). *Whole language, whole learning: Creating a literature-centered classroom*. New York: William Morrow.

Robb taps into her 30 years of experience to offer hundreds of tips to teachers as they strive to create a whole language environment. Chapters include literature response, reading experiences, and authentic assessment. Also included are 15 essays by children's authors and illustrators about the creative process.

Routman, R. (1988). *Transitions: From literature to literacy*. Portsmouth, NH: Heinemann.

> Written as a guide to assist teachers as they move away from a basal text toward authentic reading and writing, this book is filled with ideas and suggestions for using literature in the reading and writing program in the primary grades. Extensive bibliographies for professional resources, additional children's literature, journal articles, and videotapes are included.

Routman, R. (1991). *Invitations: Changing as teachers and learners, K–12*. Portsmouth, NH: Heinemann.

> Encouragement, support, and specifics on putting whole language theory into practice are the heart of this book. Routman provides specific strategies for daily management and dealing with educational issues. Nearly 150 pages of annotated resources for teachers are included.

Slaughter, J.P. (1993). *Beyond storybooks: Young children and the shared book experience*. Newark, DE: International Reading Association.

> The shared book and big book experiences are the starting point for Slaughter's hands-on approach to literacy in the classroom. Teaching tips, book recommendations, ideas for classroom organization, theme units, and shared book experiences for math, science, and social studies are included. Instructions for making big books and extensive reference lists are provided.

Stewig, J.W., & Sebesta, S. (Eds.). (1989). *Using literature in the elementary classroom*. Urbana, IL: National Council of Teachers of English.

> This book, written by well-known authorities, addresses the wide range of uses for children's literature in primary to intermediate classrooms. Uses of literature are extended throughout the curriculum to include illustrations, writing, drama, and the content areas. The book contains bibliographies of children's books and related readings.

Taylor, D., & Strickland, D. (1986). *Family storybook reading*. Portsmouth, NH: Heinemann.

Written for parents, this book explores early literacy theory as it relates to family story time. Justification for reading to young children is developed through chapters discussing why and how to share books as well as the impact of family story sharing on the child's development of reading and writing abilities. The final chapter is a guide to evaluating good books to share with young children and includes extensive book lists.

Temple, C., & Collins, P. (Eds.). (1992). *Stories and readers: New perspectives on literature in the elementary classroom*. Norwood, MA: Christopher-Gordon.

This book is organized into three major sections: theory of story meanings and reader response, using literature in the classroom, and the influence of children's development on their reading and vice versa. Topics such as the use of dialogue journals, shared inquiry, drama, making connections, growth and change in response, and culture and curriculum are discussed.

White, C. (1990). *Jevon doesn't sit at the back anymore*. Ontario, Canada: Scholastic.

White, a teacher researcher, describes her experiences of becoming a learner with her students, most particularly one student, Jevon. As White collected data through journal notes, audio and video tapes, writing samples, and photos, she began to put together a description of Jevon and his literacy experiences from the "story corner." Ultimately, she discovered that Jevon became her teacher, leading her to explore her own beliefs about teaching and learning.

Wood, K. (Ed.), with Moss, A. (1992). *Exploring literature in the classroom: Contents and methods*. Norwood, MA: Christopher-Gordon.

The notion of integration of literature across the curriculum has prompted Wood and Moss to bring together scholars from two typically distant fields, English literature and reading education. The result is a collection of chapters that discuss what to teach and how to teach it.

Areas of expertise included are multicultural awareness, technology, drama, recreational reading, and writing.

Literature Across the Curriculum

These books focus on curriculum content and describe uses of children's literature in social studies, mathematics, or science. Other works focusing on the content areas can be found under annotated bibliographies and collections.

Cullinan, B.E. (Ed.). (1993). *Fact and Fiction: Literature across the curriculum.* Newark, DE: International Reading Association.

> The recent expansion of trade books now available on many curricular topics has created a need for suggestions about classroom use. Cullinan responds to this need by bringing together children's authors and educators to explore the use of trade books in science, social studies, math, and culture. Bibliographies are included with each chapter.

Saul, W., & Jagusch, S.A. (Eds.). (1991). *Vital connections: Children, science, and books.* Washington, DC: Library of Congress.

> *Vital Connections* is designed to urge readers to consider the relationship among children, science, and books as both important and complicated. The book includes chapters by well-known science authors and educators on methods to evaluate and promote the use of children's books about science in the library and classroom. A bibliography is included.

Saul, W., Reardon, J., Schmidt, A., Pearce, C., Blackwood, D., & Bird, M.D. (1993). *Science workshop: A whole language approach.* Portsmouth, NH: Heinemann.

> A group of teachers gathered together to share their science workshop ideas. Each workshop was centered

around a theme that included children's literature. Reproducible forms and a detailed resource list are included.

Scott, J. (Ed.). (1993). *Science & language links: Classroom implications*. Portsmouth, NH: Heinemann.

This book explores the role that language plays in science learning, the ways that science can be used to develop children's language, and the relationship of knowledge about language and the development of science concepts. The book emphasizes the active involvement of children in science and language learning and is organized into three sections: science and talking, science and writing, and science and reading.

Tunnell, M.O., & Ammon, R.A. (1993). *The story of ourselves: Teaching history through children's literature*. Portsmouth, NH: Heinemann.

Focused on the need to create a history curriculum that stimulates students, this book offers support and instruction for teachers who have chosen to use trade books for this purpose. Contributors include Milton Meltzer, Russell Freedman, and Joan Blos. A section called "Practical Applications" provides in-depth examples from teachers who use literature study in their history classroom. A lengthy annotated bibliography is included.

Whitin, D.J., & Wilde, S. (1992). *Read any good math lately?: Children's books for mathematical learning, K–6*. Portsmouth, NH: Heinemann.

This book is designed to allow learners to view mathematics as a valuable, nonthreatening tool for problem solving through story. Arranged by mathematical concepts and rich in children's literature citations, this volume assists teachers as they integrate math into the classroom and daily life.

Collections of Activities and Ideas Using Children's Literature

The books in this category primarily consist of collections of lesson plans and activities, and many contain reproducible pages and ideas that quickly and easily adapt to classroom use. Although these books provide many practical ideas, they do not support teachers in developing their own theories for using literature in the classroom. The authors of these works are frequently teachers. Most include extensive bibliographies of both children's literature and professional books.

Barchers, S.I. (1990). *Creating and managing the literate classroom*. Englewood, CO: Teacher Ideas Press.

> This book is a comprehensive guide for setting up and managing a library-centered reading and writing classroom. The introduction describes whole language philosophy and practices, and chapters include summer planning, implementation, reading, writing, and poetry. Extensive bibliographies are included.

Bauer, C.F. (1993). *New handbook for storytellers: With stories, poems, magic, and more*. Chicago IL: American Library Association.

> Primarily a guide to the hows and whys of dramatic storytelling, this book includes booklists of stories for storytelling. The volume is filled with creative ways to bring children and story together through art, music, drama, puppetry, and cooking.

Borders, S.G., & Naylor, A.P. (1993). *Children talking about books*. Phoenix, AZ: Oryx Press.

> This book is structured around numerous scripted discussions between children and an adult leader about pic-

ture books. Each discussion is loosely based on three standard prompts. Author and illustrator information is included. The first two chapters contain tips and techniques for leading in-depth discussions. A useful subject index is also included.

Braddon, K.L., Hall, N.J., & Taylor, D. (1993). *Math through children's literature: Making the NCTM standards come alive*. Englewood, CO: Teacher Ideas Press.

The heart of this book is a collection of children's literature that can be adapted to NCTM (National Council of Teachers of Mathematics) standards. Chapters are arranged by standards from 6 to 13 and further divided by K–3 or 4–6 grade levels. Extensive interactive problem solving activities accompany each title. Each section is followed by more suggested titles.

Burns, M. (1992). *Math and literature (K–3)*. White Plains, NY: Math Solutions Publications.

This collection describes math lessons centered on specific children's books. Part two lists many additional titles and ideas. Many of the lessons and titles may be adapted for use in the upper grades.

Butzow, C.M., & Butzow, J.W. (1989). *Science through children's literature: An integrated approach*. Englewood, CO: Teacher Ideas Press.

The authors have selected children's literature that relates to particular science topics, and they have listed hundreds of ideas, experiments, and projects that can be used with the titles. Activities and titles related to life science, earth and space, and physical science are included.

Cairney, T.H. (1991). *Other worlds: The endless possibilities of literature*. Portsmouth, NH: Heinemann.

This practical guide for K–8 teachers who want to use literature in their classrooms includes 10 chapters of lesson plans for selected titles as well as tips for creating a literate environment. Extensive bibliographies of professional and children's titles are also included.

Coody, B. (1992). *Using children's literature with young children* (4th ed.). Dubuque, IA: Wm. C. Brown.

Written for pre-service teachers, this book is filled with ideas for using literature with children from ages 1 to 8. Chapters address read-aloud, storytelling, drama, cooking, art, and more. Extensive bibliographies follow each chapter.

Doll, C.A. (1990). *Nonfiction books for children: Activities for thinking and doing*. Englewood, CO: Teacher Ideas Press.

This collection of 57 detailed lesson plans features hands on activities with nonfiction books. Books are grouped in nine categories, including information books, biography, reference, how-to, and self-help. Grade levels are indicated, and selected titles published in 1989 in science and social studies are listed.

Fredricks, A.D. (1991). *Social studies through children's literature*. Englewood, CO: Teacher Ideas Press.

This collection of lesson plans and activities is centered around titles related to the social studies themes of self, family, community, and the world. Extensive annotated bibliographies and resource lists are included.

Fredricks, A.D. (1992). *The integrated curriculum: Books for reluctant readers, grades 2–5*. Englewood, CO: Teacher Ideas Press.

Forty different titles were chosen for their appeal to reluctant readers and included in this collection of teaching ideas. Suggestions cover all curriculum areas. Extensive bibliographies for more children's books and teacher resources are included.

Fredricks, A.D. (1993). *Involving parents through children's literature grades 3–4*. Englewood, CO: Teacher Ideas Press.

This collection of activity pages is designed to be duplicated and used in the classroom or sent home so parents can become involved with their children's independent reading. Forty children's books are featured. Each page contains summaries, discussion questions, activities, and related readings.

Goforth, F., & Spillman, C. (1994). *Using folk literature in the classroom*. Phoenix, AZ: Oryx.

The authors discuss ways to support students in their transactions with literature and then provide summaries of 54 stories from 20 countries representing 13 subgenres of folk literature. The books are arranged by theme and units for K–3 and 4–6, and instructional strategies and activities are listed. Professional references on folklore and additional bibliographies of children's books are also included.

Griffiths, R., & Clyne, R. (1988). *Books you can count on: Linking mathematics and literature*. Melbourne: Thomas Nelson.

Designed for the primary classroom, this collection of lessons uses a variety of children's literature that highlights math concepts. Rationale, classroom organization, and assessment are also explored.

Heinig, R.B. (1992). *Improvisation with favorite tales: Integrating drama into the reading/writing classroom*. Portsmouth, NH: Heinemann.

Heinig, a creative drama specialist, shares her expertise with teachers by offering some practical but substantial methods for dramatizing favorite stories in the classroom. Building on the child's natural ability to improvise, her work demonstrates that drama is a valuable medium for the study of literature and language expression.

Johnson, P. (1990). *A book of one's own: Developing literacy through making books*. Portsmouth, NH: Heinemann.

This unique book provides educators with a comprehensive guide to book art. By developing skills such as writing, story construction, design, illustration, binding methods, and paper technology, the author shows how book making can enhance many different areas of the curriculum. Full examples and step-by-step instructions are included.

Johnson, P. (1993). *Literacy through the book arts.* Portsmouth, NH: Heinemann.

This further exploration of children's literature and children's abilities with words, illustrations, and book design is appropriate for all grade levels. Using simple instructions supported with clear diagrams, the author demonstrates how scores of different book forms can be made from a single sheet of paper.

Johnson, T.D., & Louis, D.R. (1987). *Literacy through literature.* Portsmouth, NH: Heinemann.

The teaching ideas collected in this book are designed to help teachers bring literature into their classrooms. The work is organized around underlying rationale, initial literacy instruction, developing literacy, and classroom organization. The volume contains a wealth of ideas that can be readily adapted to the classroom.

Johnson, T.D., & Louis, D.R. (1990). *Bringing it all together: A program for literacy.* Portsmouth, NH: Heinemann.

In this followup to *Literacy through Literature*, the authors expand on their ideas to offer teachers a practical, classroom-tested method for integrating literature into any K–8 classroom. Advice on assessment, parental involvement, and the development of a whole language curriculum are also included.

Kelly, J. (1992). *On location: Settings from famous children's books #1.* Englewood, CO: Teacher Ideas Press.

The author has located the original settings of five popular books and photographed or drawn the homes and surroundings that are described in the literature. There are many maps and follow-up map activities.

Laughlin, M.K. & Street, T.P. (1992). *Literature-based art and music: Children's books and activities to enrich the K–5 curriculum.* Phoenix, AZ: Oryx.

The authors have developed units in art and music that incorporate children's books. Each unit includes objectives, a list of recommended readings, an introductory activity, and a list of suggested follow-up activities. Examples of unit topics are color, style, tempo and rhythm, and folk songs.

Leven, D. (1993). *Music through children's literature: Theme and variations*. Englewood, CO: Teacher Ideas Press.

Using a rich variety of illustrated folk songs, rhythmic poems, and stories with musical themes, the author introduces the topics of rhythm, melody, form, instruments, music history, and dance. Lesson plans for 40 different titles are included.

McClure, A., & Krista, J. (Eds.). (1994). *Inviting children's responses to literature: Guides to notable books*. Urbana, IL: National Council of Teachers of English.

Grounded in reader-response theory, this collection of practical ideas is intended to help teachers invite preschool through middle school readers to respond thoughtfully to books. The guides invite teachers and students to look at familiar books from a fresh perspective and come away having experienced richer, more genuine conversations with children's literature.

McElmeel, S. (1991). *Adventures with social studies through literature*. Englewood, CO: Teacher Ideas Press.

This book is a collection of literature and response activities grounded in the social studies. Chapters cover folklore, immigration, heroes, historical settings, adventure, and the history of the Newbery books. Bibliographies and two author profiles are included.

McElmeel, S.L. (1993). *McElmeel booknotes: Literature across the curriculum*. Englewood, CO: Teacher Ideas Press.

This extensive collection of teaching ideas features hundreds of children's books that can be used to teach writing, math, nutrition, and the arts. Reproducibles and recipes are included.

Mohr, C., Nixon, D., & Vickers, S. (1991). *Books that heal: A whole language approach*. Englewood, CO: Teacher Ideas Press.

Designed for bibliotherapists, this collection of lesson plans and teaching ideas is arranged by general themes of coping, death, divorce, self-concept, poverty, and others. Activities suggested for each title cover critical and interpretive thinking as well as art, drama, and creative writing.

Moss, J.F. (1984). *Focus units in literature: A handbook for elementary school teachers*. Urbana, IL: National Council of Teachers of English.

This collection of focus units uses literature as a base for theme studies and concept development. Creative writing, independent reading and creative expression are an integral part of each unit. Units include animals, the world, folktale, survival, friendship, fantasy, and more.

Moss, J.F. (1990). *Focus on literature: A context for literacy learning*. Katonah, NY: Richard Owen.

This book begins with the theoretical groundwork for literary dialogue as an aesthetic experience in the classroom. Subsequent chapters demonstrate how to use collections of related literature with children. Focus units include cat tales, wish tales, Cinderella tales, Baba Yaga tales, and more. Extensive bibliographies are included.

Moss, J. (1994). *Using literature in the middle grades: A thematic approach*. Norwood, MA: Christopher-Gordon.

The thematic units in this book are arranged in a similar format to Moss's earlier books but are focused on topics appropriate for the middle grades (4–8). Themes such as friendship stories, fairy tales, survival, family stories, war and peace, and art are developed through bibliographies, book summaries, and suggestions for dialogue and projects.

Neamen, M., & Strong, M. (1992). *Literature circles: Cooperative learning for grades 3–8*. Englewood, CO: Teacher Ideas Press.

> A project-oriented approach to using literature in the classroom, this book features 6 picture books and 26 novels. Vocabulary lists and student reproducible pages are included.

Parsons, L. (1992). *Poetry themes and activities: Exploring the fun and fantasy of language*. Portsmouth, NH: Heinemann.

> This book is organized around widely taught themes in the primary grades and uses original and reproducible poetry to begin extensive activities. A fully annotated bibliography is included.

Perez-Stable, M., & Cordier, M. (1994). *Understanding American history through children's literature: Instructional units and activities for Grades K–8*. Phoenix, AZ: Oryx.

> Each history unit of study contains annotations of fiction and nonfiction books, objectives, and detailed activities. The book is divided into units for primary and intermediate or middle school.

Thompson, G. (1991). *Choosing and using trade books in the classroom*. New York: Scholastic.

> This practical guide to using trade books in the classroom discusses choosing the right books, management techniques, reading strategies, and evaluation. Detailed model lesson plans are also included.

Author, Illustrator, and Poet Studies

These books contain biographies of authors, illustrators, and poets and lists of their works. They provide useful background information for teachers wishing to do an author or illustrator study with their students. Many contain reproducible posters of the authors and illustrators.

Copeland, J.S. (1993). *Speaking of poets: Interviews with poets who write for children and young adults*. Urbana, IL: National Council of Teachers of English.

> This book is a collection of interviews with children's poets focusing on the role of poetry in children's lives. Each interview is followed by a bibliography of the poet's work.

Cummins, J. (Ed.). (1992). *Children's book illustration and design*. New York: PBC International.

> This strikingly beautiful collection of outstanding children's book illustrations includes biographical information on nearly 80 well-known illustrators. Their insightful commentary on their work makes this an invaluable reference.

Gallo D.R. (Ed.). (1990). *Speaking for ourselves: Autobiographical sketches by notable authors of books for young adults*. Urbana, IL: National Council of Teachers of English.

> Gallo has collected and edited 87 autobiographical profiles by popular young adult and children's authors. The brief profiles include the author's life story, photographs, and a complete list of publications. Authors such as Lloyd Alexander, Judy Blume, M.E. Kerr, Walter Dean Myers, and Gary Paulson are included.

Gallo, D. (Ed.). (1992). *Author's insights: Turning teenagers into readers and writers*. Portsmouth, NH: Heinemann.

In this book, authors who write for teens offer suggestions for teachers on the value of the classics, motivating students to read, discussing books, examining issues, and the many ways to help students write effectively.

Gallo, D.R. (Ed.). (1993). *Speaking for ourselves, too: More autobiographical sketches by notable authors of books for young adults*. Urbana, IL: National Council of Teachers of English.

Gallo has again collected profiles of popular authors of books for young adults. Eighty-nine authors are featured in this volume, including Elizabeth George Speare, Lynne Reid Banks, Ursula Le Guin, and Lois Lowry.

Keifer, B. (Ed.). (1991). *Getting to know you: Profiles of children's authors featured in Language Arts 1985–1990*. Urbana, IL: National Council of Teachers of English.

Keifer has chosen a collection of articles from the "Profile" features in *Language Arts* and brought them together for this book. She includes profiles of novelists, editors, poets, folklorists, authors, illustrators, and translators that provide insight into the processes of creating children's literature.

Laughlin, J.L., & Laughlin, S. (1993). *Children's authors speak*. Englewood, CO: Libraries Unlimited.

This is a collection of speeches presented at the annual University of Southern Mississippi Children's Book Festival. The speeches span 25 years, and all the authors are recipients of the Southern Mississippi Medallion, awarded for distinguished service to children's literature.

Marantz, S., & Marantz, K. (1992). *Artists of the page: Interviews with children's book illustrators*. Jefferson, NC: McFarland & Company.

The authors interviewed over 30 illustrators of children's books, including Molly Bangs, Quentin Blake, Anthony Browne, Diane Goode, Ed Young, and Paul Zelinsky.

McElmeel, S.L. (1990). *Bookpeople: A second album*. Englewood, CO: Teacher Ideas Press.

> This second volume of the *Bookpeople* series features brief information about a wide range of authors including Lloyd Alexander, Betsy Byars, Roald Dahl, Bruce Coville, Katherine Paterson, Richard Peck, and many more. Each section contains a reproducible poster, a list of titles, more about the author, and response suggestions. The volumes in this series include authors and illustrators of picture books and books for older readers.

McElmeel, S.L. (1992). *Bookpeople: A multicultural album*. Englewood, CO: Teacher Ideas Press.

> Part of a series of books devoted to children's authors and illustrators, this volume highlights children's authors from diverse cultural backgrounds. An author poster, biographical information, description of published work, and suggestions for study and related activities are included. A cumulative index for the entire series is listed at the end of each volume.

McElmeel, S.L. (1993). *An author a month (for dimes)*. Englewood, CO: Teacher Ideas Press.

> The newest in the *Author a Month* publications, this edition features nine authors and illustrators, with three additional authors featured in capsule units. Each volume includes posters, biographies, and many teaching ideas using each person's work. Addresses and a complete list of previously featured authors and illustrators in other books in this series are included. The volumes in this series provide in-depth information on a select group of authors and illustrators.

McElmeel, S.L. (1993). *The poet tree*. Englewood, CO: Teacher Ideas Press.

> Focusing on specific poets, their lives, and their bodies of work, the author explores types of poetry, content, and other connecting threads across these poets. Biographical information and reproducible posters make this an ideal resource for poet studies.

Nodelman, P. (Ed.). (1989). *Touchstones: Reflections on the best in children's literature, Volume Three: Picture books.* West Lafayette, IN: Children's Literature Association.

> This collection of analytical essays is written by prominent individuals in the field of children's literature. Each essay focuses on one important work of a well-known author of picture books such as Beatrix Potter, Maurice Sendak, Robert McCloskey, Ezra Jack Keats, and Leo Lionni. Other volumes focus on novels and fairy tales.

Stott, J.C., & Jones, R.E. (1988). *Canadian books for children: A guide to authors & illustrators.* Toronto, Canada: Harcourt Brace Jovanovich Canada.

> A large collection of bio-critical articles on Canadian authors and illustrators, this book concludes with ideas for the classroom, a graded reading list, and a listing of titles that have received major awards.

Tuten-Puckett, K., & Richey, V. (1993). *Using wordless picture books: Authors and activities.* Englewood, CO: Teacher Ideas Press.

> This book is divided into two sections, author studies and individual title studies. The author studies include biographical information, descriptions of the author's work, and activities that feature the work to use with children. The second section has much the same format, but the emphasis is on only one or two titles by a particular author.

West, M.I. (1992). *Wellsprings of imagination: The homes of children's authors.* New York: Neal-Schuman.

> West has put together a series of essays about the homes of famous authors, complete with photographs and visitor information. He describes circumstances surrounding the purchases of the homes and the author's activities while living there. The homes of Mark Twain, Rudyard Kipling, Lucy Maude Montgomery, Laura Ingalls Wilder, and Louisa May Alcott are among the fourteen featured residences. Addresses for more information are helpful for an author study.

Wildeberger, M.E. (1993). *Approaches to literature through authors*. Phoenix, AZ: Oryx Press.

This volume is part of a series designed to motivate readers in grades 5–9. Authors are grouped by Caldecott winners, realistic fiction, fantasy, and Shakespeare, to name a few, and many teaching suggestions are included. The author approach allows students to examine style, growth, and the change writers experience over time.

Zinsser, W. (1990). *Worlds of childhood: The art and craft of writing for children*. Boston, MA: Houghton Mifflin.

In six essays, prominent children's authors reflect on their sources of inspiration in writing children's books, particularly focusing on their childhood experiences. The six authors are Jean Fritz, Maurice Sendak, Jill Krementz, Jack Prelutsky, Rosemary Wells, and Katherine Paterson.

Bibliographies of Children's and Adolescent Literature

While the majority of the professional books in all of the categories contain bibliographies of children's books, the books in this category are primarily focused on listing and organizing children's books by particular themes or topics. These bibliographies are quite extensive, and many of them are annotated with brief descriptions of the books. The bibliographies are arranged around a theme, such as disabilities, health, humor, and science, or are arranged for specific age levels or purposes, such as read-aloud, middle school readers, or young children. Some of these bibliographies begin with specific teaching strategies and rationales for their use followed by annotations of books useful for the strategy.

Barstow, B., & Riggle, J. (1989). *Beyond picture books: A guide to first readers*. New York: R.R. Bowker.

> This extensive annotated list of books meets set criteria for good first books and includes subject, title, author, readability (to 4.0), and series indexes.

Canavan, D.D., & Sanborn, L.H. (1992). *Using children's books in reading/language arts programs: A how-to-do-it manual for school and public librarians*. New York: Neal-Schuman.

> The authors' practical approach and unique organizational departure make this annotated bibliography useful for teachers and librarians. Sections include books with rhythm and rhyme, repetitive language, developing vocabulary, parts of speech, word play, and literary elements. A brief rationale introduces each section.

Carroll, F.L., & Meacham, M. (Eds.). (1992). *More exciting, funny, scary, short, different, and sad books kids like about*

animals, science, sports, families, songs, and other things.
Chicago, IL: American Library Association.

> Designed for the child user, each annotation in this collection is written in a manner that appeals to young readers. The book is arranged by categories that interest children, such as aliens, scary stories, science, and humor.

Carruth, G. (1993). *The young reader's companion.* New Providence, NJ: R.R. Bowker.

> Arranged in dictionary form, this book acquaints children with the characters, plots, authors, and illustrations in the books they read. This compendium, containing more than 2,000 entries for elementary through high school, covers topics such as literary character, mythology, classic titles, and frequently used words, symbols, and concepts.

Chatton, B. (1993). *Using poetry across the curriculum: A whole language approach.* Phoenix, AZ: Oryx Press.

> This extensive collection of poetry books is arranged around topics and includes ideas on how to share the poetry with children. Chapters cover poetry and science, math, social studies, and the language arts. Other chapters discuss thematic units, picture books, and the arts. Comprehensive lists of poems, bibliographic information, and detailed webs are included.

Cianciolo, P.J. (1990). *Picture books for children* (3rd ed.). Chicago, IL: American Library Association.

> This annotated bibliography is introduced with a lengthy chapter on choosing and evaluating picture books for children. Annotations are arranged by themes including family, others, the world, and fantasy.

Cordier, M.H., & Perez-Stable, M. (1989). *Peoples of the American West: Historical perspectives through children's literature.* Metuchen, NJ: Scarecrow Press.

> This book begins with an introduction to, and analysis of, children's historical literature of the American West. A chapter describing learning activities for developing historical concepts is followed by extensive annotations. Lit-

erature is divided by grade level and general topic. A critical analysis of the strengths of each text is included.

Estes, S. (Ed.). (1993). *Genre favorites for young adults: A collection of Booklist columns*. Chicago, IL: Booklist Publications, The American Library Association.

> This collection of annotated lists of popular reading for young adults is arranged by genres such as fantasy, romance, mystery, science fiction, and short stories.

Fakih, K.O. (1993). *The literature of delight: A critical guide to humorous books for children*. New Providence, NJ: R.R. Bowker.

> This new selection guide helps readers identify a wide range of excellent humorous books for children. Aimed at a wide audience of readers, the volume covers everything from board and picture books to young adult novels. Extensive indexes make this book easy to use.

Freeman, J. (1992). *Books kids will sit still for: The complete read-aloud guide* (2nd ed.). New York: R.R. Bowker.

> This book is divided into two major sections: interactions with children's literature and annotated read-aloud lists. The first section includes hints for booktalks and using props as well as suggestions for drama, storytelling, and 101 ways to celebrate books. The annotations are arranged either by grade level or genre. Extensive subject, author, and title indexes increase the usability of this book.

Friedberg, J.G., Mullins, J.B., & Sukiennik, A.W. (1992). *Portraying persons with disabilities: An annotated bibliography of nonfiction for children and teenagers*. New Providence, NJ: R.R. Bowker.

> This selective, annotated bibliography lists more than 350 nonfiction titles that promote acceptance and understanding of the disabled. Sensitively written and insightful essays open the work.

Hall, S. (1990). *Using picture storybooks to teach literary devices: Recommended books for children and young adults.* Phoenix, AZ: Oryx Press.

> This bibliography annotates picture storybooks according to the literary devices they contain, such as alliteration, symbolism, and tone. Specific examples of the element are highlighted in each annotation, and each is cross-referenced to other elements. The first part of the book discusses using picture books to teach literary devices.

Hayden, C.D. (Ed.). (1992). *Venture into cultures: A resource book of multicultural materials and programs.* Chicago, IL: American Library Association.

> African American, Arabic, Asian, Hispanic, Jewish, Native American, and Persian cultures are included in this book. Each section consists of a detailed bibliography (with publishers, prices, and ISBN numbers, if available) and program ideas centered around holidays and celebrations unique to the culture. Games, food, crafts, audio-visual, and adult resources are included.

The Horn Book guide to children's and young adult books. (1993). Boston, MA: Horn Book.

> Published every 6 months, this guide is an annotated, critical review of every children's book, fiction and nonfiction, published over a 6-month period. Reviews are written by prominent experts in the field of children's literature and the content areas. Extensive indexes make it easy to use.

Immell, M. (Ed.). (1992). *The young adult reader's adviser: The best in literature and language arts, mathematics, and computer science* (Vol. 1). New Providence, NJ: R.R. Bowker.

> This reference book serves as a link between subjects studied in the school curriculum (grades 6–12) and the vast array of available reading material. Profiles of famous authors precede a detailed listing of their works. Nearly 300 pages of indexes conclude the volume.

Immell, M. (Ed.). (1992). *The young adult reader's adviser: The best in social sciences and history, science, and health* (Vol. 2). New Providence, NJ: R.R. Bowker.

> This second volume of the *Reader's Adviser* covers the social sciences, history, science,and health. Extensive indexes make the volumes easy to access.

International Reading Association. (1994). *Teachers' favorite books for kids*. Newark, DE: International Reading Association.

> The children's and adolescent books annotated in this bibliography are the 1989–1993 winners of the Teachers' Choices award. This award identifies books of high literary quality that have the potential for in-depth reader response and use across the curriculum. Each year 30 books are chosen by teachers in seven regions around the United States. Annotations include a summary of the book and suggestions for using the book in the classroom.

Jensen, J.M., & Roser, N.L. (Eds.). (1993). *Adventuring with books: A booklist for pre-K–grade 6* (10th ed.). Urbana, IL: National Council of Teachers of English.

> This 10th edition of *Booklist* for elementary students features books published between 1988–1992. See earlier editions for thousands of other titles. This edition annotates nearly 2000 titles and is arranged by major categories including fine arts, historical fiction, books for young children, classics, fantasy, and much more. Each annotation includes the ISBN number and suggested age level. Author, illustrator, title, and subject indexes are included along with a list of publishers and their toll-free telephone numbers.

Kennedy, D.M., Spangler, S.S., & Vanderwerf, M.A. (1990). *Science & technology in fact and fiction: A guide to children's books*. New York: R.R. Bowker.

> This extensive annotated bibliography is arranged by fiction and nonfiction under separate science and technology headings. Each plot summary is followed by a crit-

ical evaluation designed to help users find the books that fit their needs. The subject index is a helpful guide. Reading level recommendations and ordering information are included.

Kennedy, D.M., Spangler, S.S., & Vanderwerf, M.A. (1990). *Science & technology in fact and fiction: A guide to young adult books*. New York: R.R. Bowker.

This bibliography will help teens as they search for books on science and technology that will satisfy their curiosity about space, aeronautics, computers, robotics, and more. Arranged by fiction and nonfiction, each annotation contains both a summary and evaluation. Complete buying information, a subject index, and reading levels are included.

Kobrin, B. (1988). *Eyeopeners!: How to choose and use children's books about real people, places, and things*. New York: Penguin Books.

This extensive annotated bibliography begins with sections for parents, teachers, grandparents, and librarians. Other sections include literature connections, non-book reports, and a guide to choosing quality children's literature. Many annotations include tips for using the text with children. Extensive indexes allow for easy use of this resource.

Lima, C.W., & Lima, J.A. (1993). *A to zoo: Subject access to children's picture books* (4th ed.). New Providence, NJ: R.R. Bowker.

This comprehensive index includes over 14,000 titles listed within 800 subject indexes. Listed books are further cross referenced to a bibliographic guide containing all bibliographic information and ISBN numbers for books that are new to the 3rd and 4th editions. Title and illustrator indexes are also included.

Lipson, E.R. (1991). *The New York Times parents' guide to the best books for children* (Revised and updated). New York: Times Books.

Annotated bibliography of what the *New York Times* editors believe are the best in children's literature. The text is arranged progressively from wordless books to young adult reading. Extensive indexes complete the last 100 pages.

Lynn, R.N. (1989). *Fantasy literature for children and young adults: An annotated bibliography* (3rd ed.). New York: R.R. Bowker.

This extensive volume of annotations is organized by broad categories of genre including allegory, high fantasy, magic, fairy tales, time travel, and more. The last section contains research information and bibliographies for author studies. Extensive indexes are included.

Manna, A.L., & Symons, C.W. (1992). *Children's literature for health awareness*. Metuchen, NJ: Scarecrow Press.

This annotated bibliography of children's literature deals with health issues such as nutrition, disease prevention, safety, growth and development, and family life. Early chapters discuss the evaluation of literature and integration of literature into the school health program.

Marantz, S., & Marantz, K. (1994). *Multicultural picture books: Art for understanding others*. Worthington, OH: Linworth.

Outstanding multicultural picture books are identified and critiqued for the quality of their illustrations, their reflection of the art of the culture, and their sensitivity to the spirit of the characters involved. The annotated books reflect the cultures of peoples from around the world as well as ethnic groups within the United States.

Miller-Lachmann, L. (1992). *Our family, our friends, our world: An annotated guide to significant multicultural books for children and teenagers*. New Providence, NJ: R.R. Bowker.

This comprehensive guide to multicultural literature is arranged first by the four cultures strongly represented in the United States, then by world regions. Each chapter is further subdivided by grade levels from elementary through high school. Each annotation contains a complete summary and evaluation. An extensive subject index makes this book easy to use.

The Newbery and Caldecott awards: A guide to the medal and honor books. (1993). Chicago, IL: American Library Association.

This book is an annotated guide to all the Newbery winners and honor books from 1922–1993 and the Caldecott winners and honor books from 1938–1993. The final section contains carefully researched information about the media used in each of the Caldecott works. The volume contains author, illustrator, and title indexes.

Peterson, C.S., & Fenton, A.D. (1992). *Reference books for children* (4th ed.). Metuchen, NJ: Scarecrow Press.

This annotated bibliography of children's reference books is written for school and public librarians. The work is divided into broad categories of humanities, science, social science, recreation, and general reference. The first section is a guide to the evaluation of reference materials.

Ramirez, G., & Ramirez, J. (1994). *Multiethnic Children's Literature*. Albany, NY: Delmar.

Annotations of children's literature for and about America's four major nonwhite populations, Latinos, African Americans, Asian Americans, and Native Americans, are included in this book. Each major group is divided into the different cultural groups that make up the broader ethnic category. In addition to the annotations, the authors have provided guidelines for selecting books and activities to extend the use of these books.

Rasinski, T.V., & Gillespie, C.S. (1992). *Sensitive issues: An annotated guide to children's literature K–6*. Phoenix, AZ: Oryx Press.

This annotated bibliography includes a lengthy introduction discussing how and why to use literature concerning sensitive issues with children. The detailed annotations include suggestions for further discussion. Some of the issues included are child abuse, drug and substance abuse, moving, divorce, and death. A helpful guide to publishers includes addresses and phone numbers.

Reed, A.J.S. (1988). *Comics to classics: A parent's guide to books for teens and preteens*. Newark, DE: International Reading Association.

Written for parents as a guide to support a family literacy program with young teens, this volume explores developmental issues, reading and technology, and selecting and buying books, and contains a guide to publishers. Central to the book is an annotated bibliography divided by fiction and nonfiction and further subdivided by genre or topic.

Richardson, S.K. (1991). *Magazines for children: A guide for parents, teachers, and librarians* (2nd ed.). Chicago, IL: American Library Association.

A thorough descriptive list of magazines for children, this book uses rich detail that helps the reader evaluate periodicals and make decisions for their use.

Robertson, D. (1992). *Portraying persons with disabilities: An annotated bibliography of fiction for children and teenagers* (3rd ed.). New Providence, NJ: R.R. Bowker.

This bibliography provides sensitive annotations of children's fiction focused on a wide variety of physical, emotional, and medical disabilities. Works were selected because they promote acceptance and understanding of the disabled. Grade levels are included, and an extensive subject index makes the volume easy to access.

Rochman, H. (1993). *Against borders: Promoting books for a multicultural world*. Chicago, IL: American Library Association.

This annotated bibliography of literature focuses on many cultural themes, such as immigration, family, friends and enemies, the Holocaust, apartheid, and U.S. ethnic groups. Prices and ISBN numbers are included, but publishers' addresses are not included.

Rudman, M., Gagne, K., & Bernstein, J. *Books to help children cope with separation and loss.* (4th edition). New Providence, NJ: R.R. Bowker.

> Profiled in this guide are 750 fiction and nonfiction books focusing on typical as well as traumatic childhood encounters with separation and loss. In addition to these extensive annotations of children's literature, included are articles on using bibliotheraphy to help children cope and selected readings for adults.

Schon, I. (1991). *A Hispanic heritage, series IV: A guide to juvenile books about Hispanic people and cultures.* Metuchen, NJ: Scarecrow Press.

> This book is an annotated bibliography of books for children about Hispanic people and cultures. Works are organized by country, with author, title, and subject indexes included.

Schon, I. (1993). *Books in Spanish for children and young adults: An annotated guide* (Series VI). Metuchen, NJ: Scarecrow Press.

> This annotated guide to books written in Spanish for Spanish readers is arranged first by country of origin, then subdivided by genre. The annotations are in English, and the titles and other information are translated when necessary. A guide to book dealers in the United States and overseas is included. Grade levels, price, and ISBN numbers are helpful in locating titles.

Sinclair, P.K. (1992). *E for environment: An annotated bibliography of children's books with environmental themes.* New Providence, NJ: R.R. Bowker.

> This volume contains annotations of children's books about the environment. Books are grouped by themes that include the web of life, pollution, endangered species, and food supply. Information on activities, explorations, and activism are also included. Title, author, and subject indexes are included along with interest levels and ISBN numbers.

Smallwood, B.A. (1991). *The literature connection: A read-aloud guide for multicultural classrooms*. Reading, MA: Addison-Wesley.

> The first part of this work presents necessary guidelines for reading aloud. Topics cover selection, theoretical benefits, techniques, and follow-up activities. The second contains annotations of over 260 books to share with multicultural students. Related books are listed, and extensive indexes are included.

Trelease, J. (1989). *The new read aloud handbook*. New York: Penguin Books.

> The first sections of this bibliography discuss the rationale for read-aloud, the stages of read-aloud, children and television, and the home and library. The balance of the book contains detailed annotations of books that make excellent read-alouds. Appropriate grade levels and related titles are included.

Walter, V.A. (1993). *War and peace: Literature for children and young adults*. Phoenix, AZ: Oryx Press.

> This large collection of sensitively annotated books covers many historical conflicts. The last section is devoted to books about peace, conflict resolution, poetry, and resources for adults. Grade levels and suggestions for use are included along with extensive indexes.

Webb, C.A. (Ed.)., & the Committee on the Junior High and Middle School Booklist. (1993). *Your reading: A booklist for junior high and middle school* (9th ed.). Urbana, IL: National Council for the Teachers of English.

> Organized around topics that appeal to students' interests, the bibliography contains over 1,000 annotations of titles published during 1991–1992. Earlier editions cover other years. The bibliography is arranged by categories such as love and romance, family and friends, and accomplishments and growing up. Author, title, and subject indexes are included along with publishers' addresses and toll-free telephone numbers.

Williams, H.E. (1991). *Books by African-American authors and illustrators for children and young adults*. Chicago, IL: American Library Association.

> This annotated bibliography is intended to highlight the African American experience through literature by making the literature easily identifiable. The bibliography is arranged in four major sections beginning with books for young children. The final section focuses on the work of African American illustrators.

Wilson, G., & Moss, J. (1988). *Books for children to read alone: A guide for parents and librarians, Pre-K through grade 3*. New York: R.R. Bowker.

> This annotated bibliography is arranged by grade level and readability levels. Conceptual interests such as animals and friendship guided the selection process. The volume begins with wordless books and continues through books for grade 3. Extensive indexes are included.

Wurth, S. (Ed.)., & the Committee on the Senior High School Booklist. (1992). *Books for you: A booklist for senior high students* (11th ed.). Urbana, IL: National Council of Teachers of English.

> This annotated booklist for senior high students is arranged by genre or theme. The volume includes names, addresses, and phone numbers of publishers.

Author Index

Leal, D.J., 139, 150
Lefever-Davis, S., 155
Lehman, B.A., 94, 108
Lehnert, G., 41
Lehr, S.S., 135
Leide, J., 68
Leith, R.M., 20
Leland, C., 127
Le Men, S., 54
Lemley, P.A., 146
Lenz, L., 113
Lesesne, T., 118
Lester, N., 32
Leu, D.J., 152
Leung, C.B., 114
Levande, D.I., 107
Leven, D., 235
Levine, D.M., 122
Levstik, L., 56
Lewis, M., 73
Lewis, S., 150
Lima, C.W., 248
Lima, J.A., 248
Lipson, E.R., 248
Little, G., 54
Logan, M., 32
Louis, D.R., 234
Lowe, V., 83
Lowell, J., 126
Luke, A., 107
Luke, C., 107
Lurie, A., 211
Lynch-Brown, C., 141, 208
Lynn, R.N., 249
Lytle, S., 11, 16

M

MacCann, D.C., 33, 211
MacGillivray, L., 85
Mackey, M., 48
Maclean, M., 82
MacLeod, A.S., 56
Mae, R., 36

Maher, S.N., 26
Main, I., 165
Malarte-Feldman, C.L., 56
Malecha, K., 42
Mallan, K., 88
Manhart, M.F., 50
Manna, A.L., 249
Manning, G., 73, 83, 120
Manning, M., 73, 83, 120
Many, J.E., 139, 143, 144,
    145, 146, 150, 154
Marantz, K., 239, 249
Marantz, S.S., 214, 239, 249
Maras, L., 46
Marcus, L.S., 48
Marks, P.A., 57
Marriot, S., 146
Martin, P., 72
Martin, T., 160
Martinez, M.G., 84, 86, 107,
    120, 127, 134, 153
Martlew, M., 80
Maruyama, G.M., 121
Mason, J., 86
Mason, K.M., 161
Mason, M.M., 102
McClure, A., 155, 216, 235
McClure, P., 136, 204
McConaghy, J., 104, 223
McCutchen, D., 153
McElmeel, S.L., 235, 240
McGee, L.M., 95, 160
McGee, T., 49
McGough, K., 104
McGowan, T., 104
McIntyre, E., 119
McKay, G., 114
McMahon, S.I., 140, 153,
    161
McNaughton, S., 84
McTeague, F., 224
Meacham, M.E., 166, 243
Meiners, A., 150

Pappas, C.C., 108, 125, 127, 141
Paratore, J., 83
Pardo, L.S., 140, 153
Parry, J., 223
Parsons, L., 204, 237
Pascarella, E.T., 31
Pascoe, E., 72
Paul, L., 49
Pearce, C., 228
Pearson, J., 42
Peer, G., 72
Pelland, N., 218
Pellegrini, A.D., 79, 83, 88
Penfield, E.F., 201
Penfold, K., 83
Perez-Stable, M., 237, 244
Perlmutter, J.C., 79
Person, D., 72, 100, 120
Person, D.G., 216
Peterson, C.S., 250
Peterson, R., 204
Petzold, D., 49
Phillips, A., 30
Phillips, G., 84
Phillips, J., 32
Phillips, L.M., 102
Pierce, K.M., 137, 205
Plotz, J., 63
Poe, E., 4, 5
Ponder, J.M., 141
Poole, R., 108
Porterfield-Stewart, J., 84
Pottorff, D.D., 166
Pouliot, S., 37
Prater, N.J., 85
Probst, R.E., 134, 202
Purves, A.C., 136, 205

R
Rahn, S., 26
Ramirez, G., 250
Ramirez, J., 250

Rand, M.K., 78
Raphael, R., 146
Raphael, T.E., 140, 149, 153
Rasinski, T.V., 102, 250
Rassel, M., 108
Reardon, J., 228
Reed, A.J.S., 251
Reed, S., 216
Reif, L., 224
Reimer, K.M., 25, 98
Resnick, M.B., 84
Reutzel, D.R., 128
Rice, M., 104
Richardson, A., 41
Richardson, S.K., 251
Richey, V., 241
Richgels, D., 71
Rigg, P., 36
Riggle, J., 243
Rinehart, S., 71
Rivto, H., 56
Riyne-Winkler, M.C., 101
Robb, L., 97, 224
Robertson, D., 251
Robinson, P.J., 122
Rocha, O.J., 42
Rochman, H., 251
Rogers, T., 205
Roop, P., 63
Rosenblatt, L., 198, 200, 202
Roser, N.L., 84, 86, 88, 112, 114, 115, 134, 153, 247
Ross, E.M., 25, 131
Roth, J., 84
Rottenberg, C.J., 88
Routman, R., 225
Rowland, R., 140
Rubel, S., 101
Rubio, M., 42
Rudman, M., 252
Russ, K., 73
Russell, D.L., 26, 32, 208

Sukiennik, A.W., 245
Sullivan, D.L., 20
Sullivan, J., 115
Sulzby, E., 87, 125
Sumara, D., 108
Susina, J., 49, 61
Sutherland, Z., 209
Swan, A.M., 51
Swanson, B., 71
Swanton, S.I., 121
Swift, K., 125
Symons, C.W., 249

T
Tabbert, R., 145
Tager, F., 32
Tarr, C.A., 42
Tatar, M., 49
Taxel, J., 15, 16, 216
Taylor, B.M., 121
Taylor, D., 80, 225, 231
Taylor, L.C., 48
Taylor, N.E., 81
Teale, W.H., 107, 120
Telfer, R.J., 122
Temple, C., 226
Terry, G., 160
Tetenbaum, T., 42
Thomas, M., 42
Thompson, E., 37
Thompson, G., 237
Thompson, H., 63
Thompson, L.W., 122
Thorpe, D., 50
Thuente, M.H., 50
Tiballi, B., 153
Tomlinson, C.M., 141, 208
Torsney, C.B., 28
Trachtenburg, P., 125
Trelease, J., 253
Trousdale, A.M., 141
Troxel, V., 68
Troyer, C.R., 98

Tunnell, M.O., 73, 94, 229
Tuten-Puckett, K., 241

U
Unsworth, L., 141

V
Vallone, L.M., 43
Vandell, K.S., 58
Vanderwerf, M.A., 247, 248
Vaughn, C., 140
Veatch, J., 99
Veeder, M.H., 166
Veglahn, N., 39
Vernon, J.A., 42
Vickers, S., 236
Vine, H.A., Jr., 158
Vogel, M., 35
Voss, M., 84

W
Walker, C.A., 87
Walker, J.M., 37
Walmsley, S.A., 98
Walter, V.A., 32, 253
Walworth, M.E., 109
Warren, J.S., 85
Wasserman, V., 87
Weaver, D., 140
Webb, C.A., 253
Weedman, J.E., 167
Weinstein, C.S., 120
Weir, M.N., 58
Wells, D., 157
Wells, G., 95
Wells, J., 221
Wells, M.C., 154
Wepner, S.B., 81, 221
West, J., 128, 140
West, M.I., 37, 212, 241
Westerberg, V., 68
White, C., 105, 226
White, D.R., 28, 78

White, H., 42
White, M., 47
Whitin, D.J., 229
Whyte, B., 115
Wilde, S., 229
Wildeberger, M.E., 242
Wilhelm, J.D., 154
Williams, G., 141
Williams, H.E., 254
Williams, J.A., Jr., 42
Williams, M.C., 42
Willing, K., 220
Wilson, G., 254
Wilson, P., 70, 73, 119
Wilson, R., 47
Winship, M., 128
Wiseman, D.L., 150, 154
Wishart, E., 128
Witucke, V., 56
Wolf, A., 216
Wolf, S.A., 81, 85
Wolf, V., 42
Wolfson, B., 73
Wolking, W.D., 84

Wollman-Bonilla, J., 206
Wood, K., 226
Woodard, G., 211
Woodman, D.A., 153
Woolsey, D.P., 50
Worley, S., 72
Wray, D., 73
Wunderlich, R., 57
Wurster, S., 118
Wurth, S., 254
Wytenbroek, J.R., 32

Y

Yaden, D.B., 79, 84, 85
Yandell, C.E., 28
Young, E.R., 155

Z

Zancanella, D., 106
Zarrillo, J.J., 98, 106, 151
Zielonka, P., 101
Zilboorg, C., 40
Zinsser, W., 242
Zipes, J., 18
Zipperer, F.J., 142

Subject Index

A

B

C

17–20; trends and issues in, 14–16; in voluntary reading, 116–122

D

F

G

H

HISTORICAL RESEARCH, 52–58; articles, 55–57; articles with annotations, 53–55; dissertations, 57–58

HOME: family and preschool literacy research in, 77–85

I

ILLUSTRATOR STUDIES: articles, 62–63; articles with annotations, 61–62; books, 238–242; children's literature, 59–64; dissertations, 63–64

INFORMATIONAL BOOKS: books on, 216–217

INSTRUCTIONAL STRATEGIES: literature-based approaches, 99–102. *See also specific strategies*

INSTRUCTIONAL STRATEGIES RESEARCH, 110–131; articles, 151–154; articles with annotations, 148–151; chapters, 151–154; dissertations, 128–129, 154–155; reader response, 147–155; studies, 124–126, 126–128; trends and issues in, 14

J

JOURNALS: containing research on children's literature, 190–193; featuring children's literature, 171–189; professional, 169–196; searched by hand for research bibliography, 195–196

L

LANGUAGE ARTS CURRICULUM: literature in, 218–227

LIFE CYCLES CONTENT ANALYSIS, 23, 34–37; articles, 35–37; articles with annotations, 34–35; dissertations, 37

LITERACY. *See* Family and preschool literacy

LITERARY ANALYSIS: articles, 48–50; articles with annotations, 45–47; children's literature, 44–51; dissertations, 50–51

LITERATURE: classroom, 200–202; in reading and language arts curriculum, 218–227; roles in curriculum, 93. *See also* Adolescent literature; Children's literature

LITERATURE ACROSS THE CURRICULUM: articles on, 103–104; articles with annotations on, 103; books on, 228–229; dissertations on, 104; research on, 103–104

LITERATURE-BASED APPROACHES: articles on, 100–101; articles with annotations on, 99–102; comparisons, 99–102; dissertations on, 102

LITERATURE-BASED CLASSROOMS: definitions of, 91; descriptions of, 94–99

LITERATURE-BASED CLASSROOMS RESEARCH, 90–109; articles, 97–98; articles with annotations, 95–97; books, 95; dissertations, 98–99; reviews of, 93–94, 94–99; trends and issues in, 14

LITERATURE DISCUSSION AND RESPONSE: books on, 202–206

M

MULTICULTURAL ISSUES: in children's literature, 210–212

N

NEW CRITICISM: point of view, 45

P

PICTURE BOOKS: books on, 214

POETRY: books on, 214–216

POET STUDIES, 238–242

PRESCHOOL LITERACY RESEARCH, 75–89; articles, 78–81, 81–85, 87–88; articles with annotations, 85–87; books, 77–78; chapters, 78–81, 87–88; dissertations, 85, 89; in home, 77–85; in preschool settings, 85–89; reviews of, 77

PROFESSIONAL BOOKS: on children's literature, 197–199; on sociopolitical and cultural issues in children's literature, 210–212. *See also* Books

PROFESSIONAL JOURNALS, 169–196; featuring children's literature, 171–189. *See also* Journals

R

READ-ALOUD RESEARCH, 111–116; articles, 114–115; articles with annotations, 112–114; dissertations, 115–116; reviews of, 112

READER CHARACTERISTICS, 142–147; articles on, 145–146; articles with annotations on, 143–144; books on, 143; dissertations on, 146–147

READER RESPONSE RESEARCH, 132–163; articles, 140–141, 159–161; articles with annotations, 139–140, 157–159; books, 134–137; chapters with annotations, 157–159; dissertations, 141–142, 161–162; on influence of text, 137–142; on response processes, 155–162; reviews of, 133–134; summary, 162–163; trends and issues in, 14

READING: voluntary, 116–122

READING AND LANGUAGE ARTS CURRICULUM: literature in, 218–227

READING ATTITUDES AND INTERESTS RESEARCH, 65–74; articles, 71–73; articles with annotations, 68–71; dissertations, 73–74; reviews of, 67

RESEARCH BIBLIOGRAPHY: journals searched by hand for, 195–196

RESEARCH REVIEWS. *See* Reviews of research

REVIEW AND SELECTION OF CHILDREN'S LITERATURE, 164–167; articles on, 166; articles with annotations on, 165–166; dissertations on, 166